# THE HIGH COST OF INDIFFERENCE

## Can Christians Afford Not to Act?

## EDITED BY RICHARD CIZIK

Regal Books

A Division of GL Publications
Ventura, California, U.S.A.

The translation of all Regal books is under the direction of GLINT. GLINT provides technical help for the adaptation, translation and publishing of books for millions of people worldwide. For information regarding translation contact: GLINT, P.O. Box 6688, Ventura, California 93006.

Scripture quotations in this publication are taken from the following versions of Scripture:
*KJV—Authorized King James Version*
*NASB—New American Standard Bible.* © The Lockman Foundation, 1960, 1962, 1963, 1968, 1971, 1972, 1973, 1975. Used by permission.
*NIV—New International Version,* Holy Bible. Copyright © 1973 and 1978 by New York International Bible Society. Used by permission.
*RSV—Revised Standard Version of the Bible,* copyrighted 1946 and 1952 by the Division of Christian Education of the NCCC, U.S.A., and used by permission.

This book is published by Regal Books to stimulate dialogue within the Church on issues of vital interest and concern to the Body of Christ. Not all major problems are presented here; space limitations restrict discussion within this single volume to the issues considered within these pages. Our hope is that this presentation will encourage further investigation of these and other significant concerns, and will help to replace indifference with awareness and will challenge committed Christians to direct involvement and prayerful action, thereby bringing the presence and the power of the Holy Spirit to bear on the issues of our day. The views of the various contributors, however, are their own and do not necessarily represent those of Regal Books or GL Publications.

First rights only were granted to Regal Books by Mr. Daniel W. Van Ness for the inclusion of "The Christian and the Problem of Crime—What We Can Do About It" in this collective work.

Second Printing, 1984

Published by Regal Books
A Division of GL Publications
Ventura, California 93006
Printed in U.S.A.

Library of Congress Catalog Card No. Applied for
ISBN 0-8307-1000-0

# Contents

# PREFACE

One of the most elementary biblical truths—
something everyone knows—is that God loves the world.
Any quick scan of the Scriptures confirms this. God has
shown His love for the world in sending His Son to die on
the cross for us. What most Christians fail to do is draw
out the implications of this truth. If we are to walk in
Christ's steps, we also must love the world and do so in
tangible ways. Our Lord met both the spiritual and social
needs of those to whom He ministered. And that is what
He expects of those who are called by His name in our day.

To meet these needs will require an understanding of
the theological considerations which mandate Christian
engagement in the public order. It will necessitate
thoughtful and creative alternatives in public policy. The
contributors to this book have offered many such ideas.
Because their proposals are rooted in biblical ethics, not
only believers but all citizens ought to consider them. The
views of the authors are their own, however, and do not
necessarily reflect those of the National Association of
Evangelicals or any of its member denominations,

churches or organizations. The editor has attempted to present a balanced vision, reflected in the wide range of concerns treated. May you be greatly inspired in thought and in activity by your reading and study.

—Dr. Billy A. Melvin
Executive Director,
National Association of Evan-
gelicals

# WHY THIS BOOK?

by
Robert P. Dugan, Jr.
Director, Office of Public Affairs
National Association of Evangelicals

The reporter had come to our office, just three blocks from the White House, to talk to me about evangelicals in politics. I posed what seemed to be a reasonable question: "Why is it that you have only now discovered us?"

His response was equally blunt: "Until now you haven't done anything."

He was probably right. Only recently have evangelicals entered into politics and public policy debates in any significant way. Just how much we really have accomplished is constantly being discussed on Capitol Hill and in the media.

One development cannot be denied. It is the infusion of evangelicals into the political process and their growing role in shaping public policy. We encourage and endorse this development. Why? Because, for too long, most of the intellectual public policy dialogue has lacked any evangelical element. The contributors to this book want to change all that. But to do so, they will need your help, your support, your involvement.

Our authors are surely some of the finest of the new

evangelical generation, the "first fruits" of the corrective teaching of our leading evangelical pastors and academicians who aim at developing a responsible Christian social ethic. Each writer has dealt with a different issue, and each issue demands a distinctively Christian response. Their ideas and proposals are not written for ivory-tower scholars but for thinking Christians in all walks of life.

While humbly admitting they do not have all the answers to society's ills, they are convinced of the critical need to take into government, media and the courts the implications of Jesus Christ's lordship over the whole of life. And toward this end, they have not only made the sacrifices necessary to equip themselves for the task, but they are also actively engaged in helping other Christians relate their faith to public policy. The numbers of others like them seeking to work in government are on the increase. A steady stream of them comes through the doors of our Washington office, asking for help in discovering how to penetrate the federal establishment.

**The Secular Hostility**

Evangelicals face a tough assignment. Secular minds virtually dismiss biblical values as a legitimate basis for public policy. Some are openly hostile, gratuitously tolerating religious beliefs as innocuous enough when confined to the purely personal, but off limits in the "real world."

**Our Evangelical Indifference**

There's a second reason that our task is so difficult. Unfortunately, much of the evangelical community remains on the sidelines, refusing to take an active part in public policy making. This unwillingness to engage in the battle for the very soul of our nation is not easy to accept. In some cases, it grows out of a traditional failure to understand the social implications of important theological concepts. In other cases—let us be frank—there is sinful inertia. The moral crisis in our land is the high cost of this indifference.

Am I just a dreamer? Or is it possible that Christians can make a dramatic difference in our society's moral attitudes and behavior? Quite frankly, some evangelicals are considerably less optimistic than I am on this point. They contend that evangelicals have had little effect on our culture. That may have been true, but in recent years the situation has begun to change.

## A Biblical Understanding

The marching orders for followers of Christ were laid down when Jesus said: "Render therefore unto Caesar the things which are Caesar's; and unto God the things that are God's" (Matt. 22:21). This revolutionary social doctrine has proven difficult for people to understand and apply. We all know Christians who believe there is no common ground upon which service to God and service to government can meet. They maintain that Christian faith and politics have nothing in common and ought to be strictly separate. The Church, according to this view, must confine itself to the sacred arena of life, leaving politics to the secular arena. That dichotomy runs contrary to the classic biblical understanding of the Church in the world.

## A Relevant Gospel

Some who protest Christian political involvement see it leading inevitably to compromise and a watering down of the gospel message. Their concern can be easily answered. Far from diluting the gospel, political involvement demonstrates the relevance of the gospel to the society in which we live. Not only that, but such involvement is necessary to guarantee the religious liberty which permits the preaching of the gospel. If functioning as the "salt of the earth" jeopardizes the gospel message, then Christ would not have charged us with that responsibility.

## The Appropriate Method

Of course, the Christian faith must never be confused with partisan politics or identified with a particular political party. However, risks are involved anytime moral arguments are applied to politics. For this reason, the appropriate method of political involvement is by Christians as individuals, not by churches as churches. As long as Christians individually are simply exercising their proper civic responsibilities, no one can fault them for improperly mixing religion and politics.

## The Involvement Issue

Others who protest Christian political involvement see it as violating the separation of Church and State. But that time-honored principle must never be confused with the divorcing of religious values from government. Religious values are no less valid than secular ones in a truly representative government. To ignore the biblical roots of our nation would be foolhardy in the extreme. Nowhere else can our fellow-citizens discern the criteria by which God will judge human societies.

## A Scriptural Basis

To apply the Scriptures properly to our twentieth-century government requires some study. The Old Testament was given to people living under a theocracy, but the New Testament came to people living under the heel of Rome. As different as those forms of government were, both were subject to the same divine standards of justice.

The Bible tells us that government is ordained of God to provide temporal order and justice (Deut. 16:18-20), to settle conflicts, to restrain sinful tendencies, to correct lawbreakers and to promote the public good (Exod. 18:13-26; Rom. 13:3-5). God's desire is that governments also provide for the helpless and oppressed (Deut. 15:7-11; Isa. 58:6-7,10; Ps. 72:4,12-14), avoid corruption and misuse of power (Amos 8:4-6) and respect God's lordship (Acts 4:18-20).

## A Truthful Assertion

As believers we must, therefore, recognize that government receives its authority from God and is accountable to Him. Even though others might not acknowledge God's rule over the whole of life or that ours is a nation "under God," we must as Christians assert this truth and not apologize for it. Moreover, this God is not some deistic God of civil religion, but the God of Abraham, Isaac and Jacob, who later "dwelt among us" as God incarnate. If we are to be faithful to the authority of Christ, we must extend His lordship by promoting justice and righteousness in society. That is the will of God.

## The Believer's Obligations

The Bible also establishes certain obligations for citizens toward government. The believer is to respect those in authority, obey just laws and pay taxes (Rom. 13:2-7; 1 Pet. 2:13-17). This means that we are to give honor to our leaders even though we might strongly disagree with them on some issues, and to pay taxes even though they might not be disbursed in ways which we approve.

However, if Caesar's demands contradict God's commands, we must be prepared to disobey and peaceably resist (Acts 5:40-42). We are to pray faithfully for government officials and for peace and order (1 Tim. 2:1,2). In so doing, we know that God uses world leaders for His own purposes, even when they are unaware of it (Isa. 45:5).

Finally, we owe our government the duty of service

(Titus 3:1). Service certainly includes living up to our civic responsibilities, at least voting intelligently. It is my personal conviction that this service for many Christians should include participation in the electoral process, in party and campaign activity.

## Some General Principles

Once we become involved, we must understand that the Bible is not a treatise on political theory or a manual for government. It does offer principles to guide believers but leaves the application of those principles up to the individual conscience and the public decision-making process. Some of these general principles, reflected in the chapters of this book, include: religious freedom as a God-given human right; all human life as sacred; justice within society and help for the impoverished and oppressed; dedication to peace and opposition to war; and three divinely ordained institutions—family, Church and State.

Noticeably absent from the Scripture is specific guidance on a host of political issues, as diverse as nuclear power, international monetary reform, agricultural price supports and many others. Nevertheless, if biblical principles are ignored in such cases, injustice is likely to result.

## The Agree/Disagree Dilemma

On many questions of public policy, sincere Christians will often come to different conclusions. When that happens, Christian love demands that we not engage in unbiblical accusations or recriminations over these differences of opinion. On the other hand, there are transcendant moral issues such as abortion where one should expect an evangelical consensus. There are moral absolutes!

**The Christian's Challenge**

When all is said and done, human effort will not construct the Kingdom of God. We pray, "Thy kingdom come," knowing that only Christ can bring the Kingdom to earth in its fullness. He will do that at His Second Coming.

Until then, our prayer must be "thy will be done on earth, as it is in heaven." God's answer to that prayer may well come through Christians like us. God forbid that we neglect the challenge. The cost of indifference is too high.


**About the Author**

Since 1978, Robert F. Dugan, Jr. has served the National Association of Evangelicals as director of the organization's Office of Public Affairs in Washington, D.C. He previously served 18 years in the pastorate and ran for a seat in the U.S. Congress in 1976. He is a family man and lives in Vienna, Virginia.

# PART I
## A LOOK AT THE ISSUES

# 1
# WHO IS MY NEIGHBOR?
## A Christian Response to the Poor
by
Beth Spring

One by one, churches across the country are responding to the needs of poor people in their midst as Christians discover what the Bible has to say about social responsibility. Economic and social conditions that have increased unemployment and swelled the ranks of street people have brought the problems of the poor into sharper focus in recent years. This has been accompanied by a challenge from government leaders, calling on the private sector to take charge of assisting the jobless, the hungry, the dispossessed, deserted, and victims of drug abuse and alcoholism.

They are not an attractive lot—not the sorts of people you would hurry to greet on Sunday morning if they visited your church. Consider the reception Horace might receive in a typical evangelical church. Horace had lived on the streets of Washington, D.C. for months after squandering his money, losing his job and having his car repossessed. A grizzled, unkempt black man, he lounged on heating grates and spent his days wandering in search of food.

Early one Wednesday morning, he smelled fresh coffee brewing in the basement of the Third Street Church of God. The irresistible aroma lured him inside, where he discovered other indigents eating a hot breakfast served by church volunteers. They took time to greet him and to ask about his past as they dished up a plate of eggs and biscuits for him. His willingness to pitch in and work was evident, and eventually the church offered him a job as a janitor. He readily accepted, and renewed his faith in Christ as a result of the love the people there displayed.

Horace has been on the job for three years, and lives near the church. Now he helps host the buffet breakfasts, greeting homeless drifters and letting them know there is an alternative to living on the streets, devoid of hope and a future. He did not turn over this new leaf on his own. His life was touched because a few Christians cared enough to cook breakfast for down-and-out neighbors once a week. The meal is followed by prayer, sharing, and singing in an informal setting that turns the visitor's attention toward Christ.

The Wednesday breakfast has become so popular, and has attracted so many of the city's street population, that the church has expanded the program to three days a week. It, along with a host of other neighborhood-centered ministries, is coordinated by a parachurch group, One Ministries, run by John Staggers.

Horace is only one of hundreds who pass through Third Street's door every week, and he is one of just a handful who pause long enough to detect the heartbeat of the gospel beneath the friendliness and food being offered. But numbers are not very important to the Third Street folks. They are more interested in living out a faithful response to God's claim on their lives.

## WHAT SCRIPTURE SAYS

When it addresses poverty in our midst, Scripture has plenty to say. Discovering biblical principles about poverty and the poor is as simple as turning pages—lots of them. Discerning how God's Word is meant to alter our attitudes and actions on behalf of the poor is more difficult.

Throughout the Bible, God is identified closely with the poor. Isaiah exalts God as "a refuge for the poor, a refuge for the needy in his distress, a shelter from the storm and a shade from the heat" (Isa. 25:4). And Proverbs 22:2 states, "Rich and poor have this in common: the Lord is the maker of them all." The poor are God's concern, so they are the Church's concern as well. Acting on this concern is a matter of individual calling and capability, but Scripture leaves little doubt that some response is essential.

Jesus, in one of His best-known parables, says, "I tell you the truth, whatever you did for one of the least of these brothers of mine, you did for me" (Matt. 25:40). The virtuous woman of Proverbs 31 "opens her arms to the poor and extends her hands to the needy" (Prov. 31:20).

When Christians make life more difficult for poor people, we thwart God's best intentions for ourselves and for them. "You evildoers frustrate the plans of the poor," Psalm 14:6 says. Job laments that sinful men "thrust the needy from the path and force all the poor of the land into hiding" (Job 24:4). Proverbs 14:31 assures us that "he who oppresses the poor shows contempt for their maker, but whoever is kind to the needy honors God."

The Bible makes it clear that poverty is no disgrace. It is not a punishment for sin, although it may be brought on by indulging man's sinful nature. The Proverbs repeatedly condemn laziness—or "sloth"—and indicate that poverty can be expected by those who choose a life of idleness. At the same time, Paul writes to the Romans about churches contributing money for the "poor among the saints" in Jerusalem (Rom. 15:26). Salvation did not—and does not—ensure prosperity.

Paul sets an example of good stewardship by assuring the Corinthians he has little use for material possessions. Choosing poverty as a way of life and as a testimony to God's sufficient provision has characterized the life-style of some Christians throughout church history, but it is not a requirement.

The early Church was concerned about the poor, just as God seems to be. After Paul's meeting with Apostles Peter, James and John, he wrote to the Galatians saying, "All they asked was that we should continue to remember the poor, the very thing I was eager to do" (Gal. 2:10).

In contrast, today's Christians are all too likely to fall into a middle-class American eagerness to forget the poor. Because they are isolated from us in another part of town, it is easy to compartmentalize them as someone else's problem or catalogue them with grim inner-city statistics. They are set apart, like muddied sneakers consigned to outdoor wear.

Former Congressman John Anderson has written eloquently about this mindset: "The average American today suffers no twinge of conscience when he passes the sick man on the road. He knows he has paid the Good Samaritan to come along after him and take care of this rather unpleasant social obligation. But the import of Christ's teaching is very plain. He expects us to take the role of the Good Samaritan, and not delegate our Christian love and compassion and concern in every instance to a paid professional or functionary."[1]

## IDENTIFYING WITH THE POOR

Adjusting our perspective to more closely resemble

God's view is no easy matter. Yet it requires serious consideration, because poverty is not going to be wished away, programmed away, or ignored to death.

Conservative columnist George Will notes that the "welfare state" is here to stay—a permanent fixture of national life, like the Washington Monument. The arguments society needs to be concerned with center on questions of degree (How much aid will we supply to the poor?) as well as responsibility (Who will be the provider?). Will says, "If you simply wish it would go away, then you're out of the argument."[2] His thesis is supported in Scripture.

Deuteronomy 15:11 indicates, "There will always be poor people in the land. Therefore I command you to be open handed toward your brothers and toward the poor and needy in your land." And Matthew 26:11 says, "The poor you will always have with you, but you will not always have me." The Lord, says Psalm 113:8, "raises the poor from the dust and lifts the needy from the ash heap, to make them sit with princes."

God notices the poor, agrees with them that their circumstances need improving, and exalts them to a place of dignity in society. Consider another of the Lord's statements: "I will build my church" (Matt. 16:18). Surely evangelicals, of all Christians, have taken this to heart as a mandate for coordinated, sustained evangelistic efforts.

Although, in the end, the gathering of believers will be the result of the Holy Spirit's action in individual lives, Christians are not slack about witnessing, proclaiming, and living out their commitment to Christ. We take to heart God's desire that all should be saved: we send missionaries, start Bible studies, plant churches. Above all, we encourage "life-style evangelism," allowing our witness for Christ to pervade all our activities and interactions.

A similar response to God's concern for the plight of the poor would surely involve parallel activities: feeding programs, job training, advocacy in court, along with a spiritual ministry that welcomes the poor into our midst. Perhaps it should include a commitment to "life-style social action" as well, beginning with a personal sense of identification with poor people.

Anglican author and church leader John Stott has expressed this vision for the church, presenting it in terms that synchronize well with an evangelical understanding of Scripture: "We must set ourselves simultaneously to eradicate the evil of material poverty (because we hate injustice) and to cultivate the good of spiritual poverty (because we love humility)."[3] There is an opportunity here for the church to build a bridge of compassion. Based on the similarity between how we approach Christ, and how the poor experience material life, this bridge is beyond the scope of secular understanding.

When a Christian becomes acquainted with the poor as people, he may make a remarkable discovery: They're not so different after all. Government statistics estimate that one-fourth of all Americans are "poor" at one time or another in their lives—as newlyweds, perhaps; while working their way through college, or after a temporary financial setback.[4] These people may fall below the official poverty line, but they do not lose sight of where they came from and where they are going. They retain a sense of hope for the future.

The "working poor," whose incomes hover just at the poverty line, often bear the harshest brunt of welfare reforms since they are the first to be knocked off the rolls in times of cutbacks. Yet they too have reason for optimism, especially if they have stable families and some measure of job security.

Immigrants and refugees often arrive in this country with little to call their own. Their history here, by and large, has been one of remarkable social and material success. Determination, hard work, and perseverance have characterized their endeavors. Refugees, such as the "boat people" from Southeast Asia, have achieved remarkable levels of self-sufficiency. A report completed by Church World Service, a branch of the National Council of Churches, found "the great majority of refugees are finding jobs" and their "use of public assistance is significantly lower than is commonly believed."[5]

In contrast, many of America's inner-city poor lack hope as well as material goods. Their ambition withers and dies in the "ash heap" of unemployment, inadequate education, and the debilitating cycles of drug abuse, alcoholism, and broken families plaguing their neighborhoods. Chronically poor people tend to be black, elderly, or female. Their ranks have grown in recent years because mental institutions are releasing patients who have nowhere to go, and who wind up as "street people," like Horace. Some appear to be beyond reach, refusing offers for shelter and a normal life. Yet others, like the ones God may draw to your church door, wait for someone to give them a second chance.

## THE GOVERNMENT RESPONSE

According to the government, you are poor if you must spend more than one-third of your income for food.[6] About 15 percent of America's population falls into this category, representing 34.4 million people.[7] Many of them rely on government programs—food stamps, unemployment compensation, Aid to Families with Dependent Children— to make ends meet. In 1982, a family of four with earnings under $9,862 was eligible for government assistance.[8] Their maximum monthly food stamp allotment provided about $2.10 per person per day.

Poverty became a government statistic in 1959, when the Census Bureau found that 22.4 percent of all Americans fell below a minimal income level.[9] Doctors observed symptoms of malnutrition both in Appalachia and in urban settings and a national outcry arose for relief for those people. The opening salvos of the "war on poverty" sounded, and some steady advances were achieved.

By 1965, the poverty level had dropped to 17.3 percent, and it reached a low of between 11 and 12 percent in the 1970s.[10] In 1980—the year President Ronald Reagan was elected—poverty began a slow climb and the nation entered an economic recession. Many Americans had to tighten their belts, and hard questions began cropping up: How much of the federal budget should be spent on "entitlements" to poor people? Do these welfare programs destroy incentive, locking poor families into generations of misery? What are churches, corporations, and charitable organizations doing to address the problem?

The Reagan administration has veered from the course set by theorists of the 1960s by sharply curbing the growth of government assistance programs. On these proposals, he has met with considerable cooperation from Congress. Other ideas, such as turning welfare over to the states and requiring welfare recipients to work for the benefits, have foundered on Capitol Hill.

To help government planners grapple with ways to streamline the federal response to poverty, staff members of a House of Representatives subcommittee developed six principles to guide the process.[11] They indicate the complexity of the process and are worth examining in detail:

1. *Fairness.* People in similar circumstances should be assured similar treatment despite different eligibility rules and benefit allotments from state to state.
2. *Adequacy.* The report asks, "At what level of living is society as a whole willing to maintain its poorest members?" Along with this very difficult social

judgment is an even thornier problem: The more "adequate" a government program is for some people, the less "fair" it is for those who are barred from it.

3. *Target Efficiency*. Should benefits be conferred most generously on poor people who can work, or on those who do not work? While it may seem logical to channel limited funds to those who need it most because they have no other income, this has the unintended effect of destroying the incentive to work.

4. *Work Incentives*. When a poor person's income goes up, even slightly, his noncash benefits—such as food stamps—may be reduced as a result, leaving him no better off.

5. *Family Stability*. "A system of help for the poor should encourage two-parent families to stay together," the report states. Presently, most states confine welfare benefits to one-parent families or those with an incapacitated second parent, making it financially rewarding for families to split.

6. *Cost*. As if the preceding concerns were not enough, most of them also require additional cost to ensure that they are working.

As these components suggest, federal antipoverty efforts consist of a vast, intricate webbing of ideals and hard realities. The "safety net" image often employed to describe these programs is remarkably apt.

## The Fairness Debate

The current debate over cutting back these programs reflects two underlying philosophies that guide policy making in Washington. The government, particularly under conservative leadership like that of President Reagan, uses an "absolute" definition of poverty. When he speaks of the "truly needy," he is referring to people whose income falls below an arbitrary line that changes with the ups and downs of inflation. Conservatives would expect the number of poor to decline during times of healthy national economic growth, and to rise during times of slow growth or recession. Their emphasis on intangible "free market" factors, rather than direct assistance, often leads to accusations that they are insensitive to the poor or lack compassion.

Critics of the Reagan approach view poverty in "relative" terms, believing that poverty means having a lot less than most people have. According to a report prepared for the U.S. House of Representatives Ways and Means Committee, proponents of this position reject economic growth as a sufficient cure for poverty. "Under a relative standard," the report says, "poverty would be reduced only if income became distributed more equally."[12]

Reagan believes that economic growth will provide the best hope for the poor in the long run. One critic has replied, "The problem is that a child does not eat in the long run. And an elderly person does not have a long run."[13] Others question the very basis of Reagan's position, saying the limits to economic growth are rapidly being reached, while natural resources are becoming more scarce.

Conservatives believe that the poor will be motivated to work harder if it becomes more difficult to receive welfare benefits. Liberals say the poor are in no position to take advantage of new opportunities—such as high-tech computer jobs—because they lack education and skills. While Reagan believes the private sector needs to exert more effort on behalf of the poor, his critics reply that those private sources of assistance have reached and exceeded their capacity to help.

The media term this debate "the fairness issue," and

that phrase should set off alarm bells inside the heads and hearts of Christians familiar with Proverbs 31:9: "Speak up and judge fairly; defend the rights of the poor and needy." On which side of this complex issue do Christians belong? Increasingly, Christians are aligning themselves with one side or the other.

At the liberal end of the spectrum, the focus is on government responsibility, limits to growth, and the rights of the poor to be full participants in society. These theorists are suspicious of an unrestrained free market economy, believing that without a boost from the government, the poor will perpetually remain at the bottom rung of society's ladder.

Christians who take this position cite theological reasons for it. Ronald J. Sider, author of *Rich Christians in an Age of Hunger,* believes the doctrine of original sin requires restraints on the pursuit of wealth, since man— left to his own devices—is unlikely to be generous toward the poor. "One of the very powerful, constant themes of the Bible is that God is on the side of the poor. He wants redistribution so the poor can participate. The effect of Reagan's policies has been to shift resources from the poor to the rich. That is fundamentally opposite of what Scripture calls for," Sider says. [14]

One example of this is a recent shift in the relationship between the income tax threshold and the poverty line. A report from the congressional Joint Committee on Taxation points out that since 1981, more and more people with incomes below the poverty line have been subject to federal taxation. In the 1970s, when inflation brought on this contradictory gap in government policy, tax cuts were structured to shield the poor from owing money to the same government that was handing out welfare benefits to them. [15]

Moderate Senator Mark O. Hatfield questioned the

virtues of economic growth in a 1980 article in *Christianity Today:* "That growth has not yielded the results of social harmony, economic justice, and personal fulfillment it promised. It has not solved the issue of justice, either at home or around the globe. The gaps have increased and the poor have been left on the bottom."[16]

Since that article appeared, a sophisticated economic apologetic has developed on the right. Conservative George Gilder, in particular, has framed the "fairness" issue in distinctively theological terms, rebutting the major arguments put forward by Sider, Hatfield, and others.

Gilder, whose book *Wealth and Poverty* has influenced Reagan administration policy, defends letting "the rich get richer" because he says they are "fostering opportunities for the classes below them in the continuing drama of the creation of wealth and progress."[17] He identifies "work, faith, and family" as the three requisites for wealth in American society and harshly criticizes liberals for discounting the importance of these facts of life.[18]

Like countless immigrants who have achieved prosperity, he says, the poor need poverty to be a spur toward self-improvement rather than a condition that is rewarded and perpetuated. "The crucial goal" of welfare reform, he says, "should be to restrict the system as much as possible by making it unattractive and even a bit demeaning."[19]

In addition, Gilder and his compatriots dismiss warnings about the "limits to growth." They count on human ingenuity and untapped, undiscovered resources to combine endlessly in providing new opportunities. Recent development of the microchip, which has revolutionized computer usage and opened sweeping vistas of business and personal application, is frequently cited as an example of how unanticipated forward leaps of knowledge can change our daily lives.

Catholic author Michael Novak sums up the views of the free-market boosters in *The Spirit of Democratic Capitalism:* "Those who lack opportunity for self-advancement have a legitimate grievance against its (society's) promises. Those who can demonstrate unequal results have no such legitimate grievance. A free society is necessarily committed to unequal results."[20]

But other theorists say the Bible calls us to be aware of unequal results and to work to reduce them. Ron Sider writes, "Over and over again God specifically commanded his people to live together in community in such a way that they would avoid extremes of wealth and poverty. That is the point of the legislation concerning the Jubilee and the sabbatical year. That is the point of the legislation on tithing, gleaning, and loans. Jesus, our only perfect model, shared a common purse with the new community of his disciples. The first-century Christians were simply implementing what both the Old Testament and Jesus commanded."[21]

Conservatives, therefore, envision a society of people walking parallel routes along the road of opportunity. Some will inevitably fall behind while others quicken their pace and endure all the way to the finish-line of prosperity. They are blazing trails in which the poor will eventually follow, conservatives say. Meanwhile, the swifter travelers occasionally need to give a lift to the ones lagging behind. This is charity—a temporary solution to a problem that will resolve itself naturally down the road.

Liberals, in contrast, challenge society's affluent members to stop being preoccupied with personal prosperity and focus instead on their fellow travelers. Slow your pace, they would say, so the people without all your advantages in life have a chance to catch up. Don't just give the unfortunate ones a grudging free ride to the next corner; see to it that their feet can be shod as handsomely as your own so they can compete with a reasonable chance of success.

On both sides, policy makers and social theorists realize it is vitally important to narrow somehow the gap between rich and poor. George Will explained in an interview why this matters to him: "I have three children growing up in Chevy Chase. There are children growing up 10 miles away in Anacostia (a poverty-stricken neighborhood in Washington, D.C.). They're both Americans, but they have almost no common experience. That's worrisome, and it ought to be especially worrisome to a conservative, because conservatives are nationalists. They say we all ought to be Americans, to share certain values, and to feel positively about the community. But what does my child have to say to the child in the slum? It's very hard."[22]

The solution, Will says, is far from clear. "But whatever it is, it is not to deny that it is a problem." The shared American goal of equal opportunity is complicated by a multitude of external factors: the quality of urban schools; prenatal care; nutrition; racism. Will, departing from some of his conservative colleagues on this point, argues that "equality of opportunity" is a product government has to provide.[23]

## HOW CHRISTIANS ARE RESPONDING

People who differ philosophically on this issue tend to share at least one common bond: a belief that the private sector—and particularly the Church—has a crucial role to play. Conservative U.S. Senator Jesse Helms has promoted private initiatives during hearings on Capitol Hill, stating, "Most churches have a far greater capacity to help their neighbors than they have been willing to assume." He even has cited his own Baptist church in North Carolina for failing to do more than deliver a basket of food to a poor family on Thanksgiving.[24]

Senator Hatfield frequently notes a study conducted by his staff, who found that welfare rolls would dwindle substantially if every U.S. church "adopted" one or two poor families to care for. That day appears to be a long way off, but the ways in which some churches and individual Christians are tackling problems of poverty provide some encouraging insight into the rewards and results of personal involvement. There are large-scale, well-known efforts as well as quiet, unsung examples that touch just a handful of lives.

Barbara Connell attends a Washington, D.C. church near Capitol Hill, where Senate staffers and welfare families live near one another in row houses. Connell, deeply moved by seeing ghetto teenagers ruin their lives by dropping out of school and taking drugs, began tutoring grade-school children from a nearby school. "It's a ministry that's developed simply because I love the kids and don't want to see them on welfare or using drugs when they get older," she says. To encourage them to improve their reading skills and engender pride in achievement, she developed one-page biographies of famous black Americans because the children "have few positive role models."

Connell's approach to poverty, in this case, is a simple, service-oriented labor of love. She views her 15 students as individuals, who, like anybody, just need some assurance and assistance toward leading productive lives.

In Mississippi, John Perkins has developed a community-based approach to poverty through Voice of Calvary Ministries. This seasoned Christian activist identifies "three Rs" for neighborhood improvement in depressed areas: relocation, reconciliation, and redistribution. "Poverty is the lack of options," Perkins says.[25] He believes that Christians who want to provide the poor with increased options for successful life choices need to consider relocating—living in the midst of those they seek to help. Reconciliation is a process leading to identification with the poor person—despite his color or condition—as a friend, neighbor, and equal. Finally, ensuring that justice is served means redistributing the resources God makes available to us.

These principles are being tested in New York City by Campus Crusade for Christ in a new program called "Here's Life Inner City." Located in the squalor of Times Square, this ministry effort began with a commitment to build solid bridges of trust and cooperation with local church efforts to shelter the homeless and provide day care for working mothers. It reflects a shift toward a "relational, not programmatic" approach, according to a spokesman.

World Relief, the development, relief, and refugee assistance arm of the National Association of Evangelicals, is beginning to channel resources to the American poor as well as to dependent newcomers from abroad. In an Atlanta program, World Relief has linked 12 churches in partnership with 36 welfare recipients, with the goal of seeing them build job skills and gain employment as soon as possible. Also in Atlanta, Evangelicals for Social Action helped to purchase run-down homes near the airport. They are fixing up the houses to rent out at very low cost to poor families.

In Chicago, Salem Evangelical Free Church provides English-language classes and an informal job-placement service for Hispanic immigrants. Their bilingual pastor, Doug Moore, was raised on the mission field in Chile. As the neighborhood blocks surrounding Salem began changing from a concentration of European ethnic groups to an Hispanic majority, the church adjusted its ministry emphasis to suit the newcomers' needs. Moore has discovered that his Hispanic members are industrious and family-centered. "I admire these people," he said. "Their average income is $4 or $5 an hour, and still they manage to send money home each week to Mexico or Puerto Rico."

Routine household repairs or emergencies may be catastrophic for a person whose income barely covers the necessities. Fourteen churches in Portland, Oregon, discovered they could combine their resources to meet day-to-day special needs of the working poor. "Reach Out" matches requests for car repairs, babysitting, transportation, tutoring, fix-up chores—among others—with the skills and abilities of Christian volunteers.

In each of these cases, church people are providing a personal touch that government programs are not equipped to give. Christians in these and many other communities began by learning what the Bible teaches about caring for the poor and needy. They turned their attention to pressing local problems and tailored a response to fit specific needs. They might disagree on the theoretical aspects of alleviating poverty, but that has not prevented cooperation and initiative on behalf of their neighbors.

The poor, like the wounded man the Good Samaritan helped, have a legitimate claim on some of the resources God entrusts to us. "Who is my neighbor?" is a question Christians need to ask thoughtfully and prayerfully. The follow-up to this question is important, too: "What does God want me to do for my neighbor?"

John Anderson tells the story of a church in Germany which was destroyed during World War II. As the rubble was cleared away, a statue of Christ was found with the hands missing. "A famous sculptor offered to restore the hands, but the officers of the church declined, saying that this was a symbol of our Lord's dependence on the hands of His followers to serve Him in loving concern and compassion for others."[26]

What has the Lord placed within your reach that could meet the needs of the poor? For the volunteers at Washington's Third Street Church of God, it was a hot breakfast platter. Other hands are busy making phone calls, sorting donated clothing, or pointing out unfamiliar English words on a blackboard. Sometimes the Lord has need of an empty pair of hands as well, to console someone who is distraught about being unable to provide for a growing child.

Often, Christians who are willing to help do not know where to begin, since they are not personally acquainted with the poor and needy. They may begin by praying to a God who is intimately acquainted with the less fortunate, and asking for the privilege of making a difference in someone's life. Jesus said, "For I was hungry and you gave me something to eat, I was thirsty and you gave me something to drink, I was a stranger and you invited me in, I needed clothes and you clothed me, I was sick and you looked after me, I was in prison and you came to visit me" (Matt. 25:35-36).

---

## Study Questions

1. Read Isaiah 25:4; Proverbs 22:2; Galatians 2:10; Matthew 25:40; and Proverbs 31:20. Discuss the ways in which God—and godly people—identify with the poor.

2. Compare "the evil of material poverty" with "the good of spiritual poverty." How are these conditions similar? How do they differ?

3. How much of your income do you spend on groceries? How would your life be different if your food bill consumed 1/3 of your take-home pay? What sorts of meals could you prepare for your family if you could spend only $2.10 per person per day?

4. How does healthy economic growth help the poor? In what ways might it hurt them?

5. List the factors that affect a person's chances of "getting ahead" in society, such as talent, schooling, etc. Why is it so difficult to ensure "equal opportunity" for everyone?

6. Keeping the poor in mind, how would you answer the questions, "Who is my neighbor?" and "What does God want me to do for my neighbor?"

7. If you are not acquainted with any poor people, how could you set about meeting and identifying with them?

## Suggested Readings

Davis, John J. *Your Wealth in God's World.* Phillipsburg, NJ: Presbyterian and Reformed Publishing Co., 1984.

Novak, Michael. *The Spirit of Democratic Capitalism.* New York: Simon and Schuster, 1982.

Perkins, John. *With Justice for All.* Ventura, CA: Regal Books, 1982.

Sider, Ronald J. *Rich Christians in an Age of Hunger.* Downers Grove, IL: Inter-Varsity Press, 1977.

Will, George F. *Statecraft as Soulcraft: What Government Does.* New York: Simon and Schuster, 1983.

## About the Author

Beth Spring is Washington Correspondent for *Christianity Today* magazine, a position she has held since 1981. Her research on poverty has produced a cover story for

*Christianity Today,* "Is There Hunger in America?," as well as articles for *Brigade Leader, Evangelical Newsletter,* and *HIS* magazine. Beth is a graduate of Northwestern University's Medill School of Journalism.

# 2

# RECONCILIATION AND INVOLVEMENT
## A Positive Approach to the Media
by
John Rodman

In 1976 Jimmy Carter scored a surprise victory in the
New Hampshire primary, or so the newspapers announced
the following morning. And having been crowned by the
media, he was then challenged to survive the grilling of
reporters from that day forward.

The morning after his New Hampshire victory he met
with reporters in Boston to begin his run for the next hur-
dle, the Massachusetts primary, then a week away. Jack
Cole, of WBZ-TV in Boston opened the session by asking,
"Governor Carter, now that you have won the New
Hampshire primary, will you become specific on the
issues?"

Carter flashed his now famous smile and replied that
he had been specific on the issues all along. He went on to
add, "The voters of New Hampshire know where I stand
on the issues, and that I am running an open and intimate
campaign. When I am elected president, I will be open and
intimate with the American people."

I interrupted Jack Cole's next question to ask, "Governor, how can you seriously say you will be intimate with

220 million Americans?"

Carter smiled again, and answered, "Well, it all begins with the accurate reporting of news conferences."

This polite minuet between candidate and reporters suggests something about the crisis in American journalism today. No president, and only a few candidates since the days of John F. Kennedy have expressed the belief that they have been treated fairly by the press. Today the majority of Americans not only have the same doubts but their concerns are becoming wider, touching on the whole range of the arts and media in America.

Interestingly, some in the media are beginning to criticize other elements of the media for failing to meet a presumably common standard of social responsibility. A major weekly women's magazine ran a cover story asking, "Does Hollywood Care What It Is Teaching Our Kids About Life?" The article accused the makers of summer teen movies of depicting sexuality in terms which deny most of the basic values of our society.

Even major newsweekly magazines have devoted cover stories to examining what is wrong with the press. And opinion surveys show the American public puts journalists way down the ladder in terms of confidence and reliability.

## ARE THE MEDIA BIASED?

Let's briefly consider some of the charges the public levies against the media. The news and entertainment media are often accused of covertly choosing sides in political and social debates in our nation while claiming to fairly and accurately depict our world.

There is more than sufficient evidence to support that charge of bias even in the more established and prestigious publications and broadcasts. A fascinating bit of evidence of this is the decision by The Newspaper Guild, a writers' trade union, to endorse Walter Mondale for the Democratic presidential nomination almost 10 months before the 1984 Democratic Convention. While Guild President Charles Perlick, Jr. was criticized by some of the move, the endorsement was not repudiated.

On the other side, The Wire Service Writers Guild refrained from taking partisan political action. However, the charge of being wedded to an ideology and one particular political party has raised severe questions about journalistic integrity.

Coverage itself is sometimes compromised by political bias. The Associated Press has openly admitted that one of its reporters falsified a story about the nuclear freeze. The reporter, covering a congressional hearing investigating the nuclear freeze and the evidence of Soviet covert funding of that campaign in Europe, incorrectly reported that the administration's spokesman at the hearing contradicted President Reagan's charge that the Soviets had been caught red-handed by NATO governments delivering hundreds of thousands of dollars to pro-unilateral disarmament groups in Europe. What in fact transpired was testimony indicating that there is insufficient evidence to demonstrate that any of that money had reached pro-unilateral disarmament groups in the United States. That statement was indirectly cited as a contradiction of the President's position, but neither the testimony nor the President's actual words were quoted.

The media, both news and entertainment, are also accused of deliberately smearing the evangelical community. There are allegations of distorted reporting of the statements of evangelical leaders. Conversely, the media is accused of covering up information which is inconsistent with its views.

The inevitable problem with all these charges is that they apply in certain specific situations, such as the cases cited. But it is not fair to characterize the entire creative community, and professional journalists in particular, by such charges. There is a need to be careful and cautious when considering the behavior of the people in the communications industry. Just as there are more and less mature people in the church, likewise there are more and less mature people in the creative community.

Nevertheless, we are acutely aware that something is wrong, but we do not know what. The U.S. Surgeon General has suggested an interesting possibility. In remarks made on the issue of television violence, Dr. C. Everett Koop has noted that a growing and impressive body of research links violence in the community to the home where violence is viewed on the tube. Yet even if one TV station took it off the air, another would merely increase it. The viewers, Dr. Koop concludes, would indeed turn to the violent programming. If TV violence is in fact killing us, why do we keep watching it? And who is more to blame? Only the media?

Dr. Koop, among others, is increasingly convinced that the real problem lies elsewhere. He advocates more research on the issue.

## IS THE MEDIA RELIGIOUS?

A survey conducted by a public opinion magazine reports some curious statistics about the attitudes of key decision-makers in American media, as compared to the public at large. The survey examined the attitudes of a sample of writers, directors, producers and other key decision-makers in the entertainment media. It found they were two to four times more likely to approve of such things as homosexuality, legalization of some drugs, casual sex outside of marriage and abortion on demand than the average American.

On the other hand, the average American is three to

five times more likely to be a regular church-goer or church member than the so-called media elite. Only about 10 percent of the key opinion leaders in the media interviewed for the survey said they go to church or synagogue regularly. And almost as many expressed outright hostility toward religion and religious values.

A large percentage say their parents were religious or that they were raised in a religious home, but that they themselves have moved away from church and synagogue. Jews and Gentiles alike expressed equal ambivalence or antipathy toward religion.

What does this mean? It would be easy to point the finger at the creative community and say with self-righteousness that they are more depraved than the rest of us. It *would* be easy. But it would not be correct.

## IS THE CHURCH INDIFFERENT?

Rather, what this survey reveals is the withdrawal of the Church from the creative community. The Church has abdicated its role. It first abandoned film, then radio and television. The very forms themselves were described as inherently evil. Yet St. Paul says explicitly that nothing, in and of itself, is evil. It is man's use and abuse of creation which produces evil. If there is excessive depravity, that is the predictable effect of the Church's indifference.

Chuck Colson reports a curious encounter with a network TV executive, who noted with some evident satisfaction that when a rival network had run the immensely successful film, *Chariots of Fire,* it had finished dead last in the ratings. He asked Colson, "So where were the Christians?"

While the TV executive's remark betrays a certain bias, and his argument contains more than a few flaws, his point is still well taken. Where are we indeed? And what do we know of the real world in which TV, film and radio professionals live and work? Could we do any differently and any better than they?

The media in America are like every other enterprise—they are a business. Shows are produced to draw an audience in order to offer goods for the consumers' consideration. The American media is a very high-pressure, high-budget industry. The stakes are immense, the rewards great and the consequences of failure equally great.

TV stations in major American markets now receive audience rating reports each and every day. How would you like to come to work each day and find yesterday's work graded, in segments a quarter of an hour at a time, and compared with every one of your competitors? And remember that they are looking at the same grade sheet you are at the same time.

When it comes to hard news reporting, deadline pressures complicate the picture. In radio the next deadline is never more than 55 minutes away. In television the deadlines run between six and eight hours while the longest newspaper deadline is 12 hours, although most are far less.

How many Christians understand how the news system works? How many can even define news, explain how it comes into being or how it makes its way to TV or into the newspaper? How many Christians understand the legal framework of our free press and which issues are central to the functioning of that press (electronic and print) in the last quarter of the twentieth century?

Many will reply that we need not know any of the above to know we are not fairly depicted in the news media. True enough. But what then is the point of criticism—to correct or to denounce? If our criticism is uninformed, we are doing nothing more than making shrill noises for our own satisfaction.

We have a responsibility to become more informed and active in the news system if we are to make a meaningful contribution. In light of the Great Commission we can do no less, for Jesus said we are to go and make disciples from among all nations (see Matt. 28:19-20). If we, through our inactivity, permit the world to have a distorted view of us, we are in part responsible for their rejection of the God we serve.

## CAN CHRISTIANS BE A PART OF THE MEDIA?

There is something which can be done. It is possible for Christians to have positive relationships with major news organs. It is also possible to assure accurate coverage, adequate information and even a friendly reception in news rooms and air studios. Such was the case in Boston, Massachusetts when a pilot project was conducted in 1980 by the Evangelistic Association of New England (EANE).

A need was identified: news editors, writers, anchors, producers and reporters in the Boston area were regularly asking (before going on the air or into print) for information, referrals, advice on accuracy and general feedback on current as well as future stories. These were the kinds of services resulting from 18 months of work by the Evangelistic Association of New England. And the results were gratifying. WBZ-TV of Boston has called the work of EANE's press office "the best in ten years" in any field of community or public relations in Boston. Other stations in Boston have called the work of EANE "invaluable," "outstanding" and "exciting."

What brought this kind of response from radio, TV and newspaper people? Don Gill, executive director of the Evangelistic Association, began by hiring a professional broadcaster and journalist who had not only spent eight years in Boston radio and TV but was also an evangelical capable of representing the Association and the Christian community. The basic philosophy of the program is summed up in Max Ways' famous comment in *Fortune* magazine: "Public relations proceeds from a respectful and even humble recognition that we need to explain ourselves to people we can no longer ignore or coerce."

The Public Affairs program of EANE began with extensive research on the fabric of radio/TV/newspaper organization in Greater Boston. The Association then sent out several releases explaining the program, along with resource materials published by the Association. These materials included a regional church resource book with complete listings for all denominational, non-affiliated and para-church programs in the New England region.

Using standard news releases, the Association then began raising issues and making spokesmen available on those issues. Each release was carefully prepared to conform to the conventions of style and attribution in use in the Boston market. Copy was written specifically in broadcast format and each story was geared to "bounce off" current news, especially from a local and preferably non-religious angle.

The result was dozens of interviews, programs and news stories on all three network-affiliated TV stations in Boston, along with the top three stations in Boston radio. One success story involved a 15-minute interview with the CBS-owned and operated all-news station, WEEI. The Association had just completed research on church growth in the Cape Cod region of Massachusetts. News releases were then sent to over 100 news outlets in New England. WEEI responded, making time available for an interview with Association field representative, the Reverend Paul A. Johnson. The interview, played during the newsline segment, reached an estimated audience of 65,000 listeners.

Several one-hour programs, produced as a result of

EANE stories, were aired by independent and network-affiliated TV stations in Boston. One particular program, a prime-time consumer show called "Money Sense" (8:00 P.M. Wednesday, on NBC's WBZ-TV), prepared an 11-minute segment on evangelicals working in the business community. Prompted in the beginning by an unfavorable article found in the *Los Angeles Times,* the "Money Sense" producer contacted EANE. The choice to work with EANE was based on previous news releases which had crossed her desk. EANE contributed heavily to research-ing the piece and there was only *one* negative comment in the entire 11-minute segment. Other programs produced as a result of EANE stories dealt with politics, national defense, abortion and creationism.

The key to the process is the personal trust relation-ship built up with news people. The Association did not take an advocacy posture vis-a-vis reporters, but assumed a resource posture instead. The Association openly sought to discover and meet the needs of producers, reporters and others.

During the entire process EANE kept in mind the fact that radio, TV and newspaper enterprises are businesses. They require lively, animated and interesting content to get and hold audiences. Confrontation with news people is avoided, except where there is no choice (an eventuality which never materialized).

The Association tried to cultivate relationships which encouraged reporters to trust the information it provided and to use it accurately. In one particular instance the Association provided information to a *Boston Globe* reporter which, if printed out of context, could have been very damaging to the Boston Roman Catholic Archdio-cese. However, the reporter printed the data with all the appropriate limitations, quoted exactly from the disclaimer and presented all information within the proper context.

This seems to stand in sharp contrast to the perception that the news media is inflexibly biased against the evangelical community. Why the disparity? Why did one organization enjoy such a warm relationship with, and in access to the news media, when so many other evangelical organizations do not? It is necessary to understand even more about news and its environment.

## IS THE CHRISTIAN PERSPECTIVE OF THE MEDIA CORRECT?

Many people believe that the news media purports to be neutral. The quest of the journalist is not for neutrality but balance. No one article can fully touch more than one side of an issue. This is why major stories are covered day by day and often by more than one reporter, rather than in one comprehensive item written after the conclusion of the story. The reporter gathers all the information available, sifts it, and reconstructs the story into a distillation of the real event using the medium at hand—either video, radio or print. Journalists also have opinions and express them in columns and editorials. This is an imperfect process, but it is the best available.

There is a second myth, which is the more pervasive and perhaps the most destructive of all—the myth that reporters and their editors are the entire newsgathering system. This is not the case. There is an enormous interlocking network of reporters and their sources which makes possible the news system as we know it and all nations and societies have such interlocking relationships. The differerce between a free press and a controlled press involves who it is that decides what goes into print—the reporters or their sources.

In the United States reporters interact with political and corporate leaders, educators, industrialists, businessmen, community service leaders, special interest groups, and people on the receiving side of news. All of the individuals in these categories who communicate their interests accurately employ people who understand the news media and know how to communicate with the people in news organizations.

There is a substantial trust relationship between these people and the writers and reporters they serve. This relationship is based on accuracy and an understanding of the respective roles of each participant. Reporters have the final say on what they write and should not be criticized for not taking a particular point of view and swallowing it whole. Reporters, on the other hand, understand that press spokesmen are responsible for presenting their case in the best possible light. Each takes the judgment of the other with a sense of fairness and enough skepticism to keep a clear perspective. When reporters and their sources both respect and deal fairly with one another, the system works very well indeed.

## HOW DOES THE CHURCH REPRESENT ITSELF?

Imagine a situation, however, where the reporter has no contact person or where a contact is uncooperative, silent or openly hostile. Not much communication takes place. Imagine an entity so fragmented and decentralized as to have literally hundreds of voices, all claiming to speak authoritatively for the whole. Consider an institution where rivals have attempted to use reporters to besmirch one another in their intramural rivalries. How does a reporter, who has little or no experience with such an entity, make sense of it all (especially since the institution in question uses a language distinctive from common English)? How would you report on such an entity? And how would you respond if you were then described as biased, uninformed and hostile to the institution?

This is the experience of most secular reporters when

they have covered the Church. Untangling the maze of competing theologies, ecclesiologies, forms of government and their respective vested interests is all but too much for most reporters. We must educate ourselves on the mechanisms of good news relations, understanding the pressures on reporters, editors, and their co-workers. Making their jobs easier, not harder, will begin the process of proving that we are people of love, not manipulators or power seekers. If we honestly seek to serve their needs, they will be sensitive to ours. But we must take the first steps.

## HOW SHOULD THE CHURCH REPRESENT ITSELF?

Any kind of work with large media outlets, metro TV, radio or newspapers must be done from a regional organization. Individual churches are not in a position to work with major market media outlets because each church represents only one part of the evangelical constituency. Stations would be besieged by every church in their coverage area if they put only a couple of churches on the air.

An experienced news person must be secured to do the work. This is not public relations or pastoral ministry. Working in the news environment is a very complex task. It requires experience and confidence. Reporters and producers work under enormous pressures because of the deadlines and the huge sums of money involved in their work. Anyone who works with radio, TV or newspapers must understand the pressures and be able to confidently cope with them.

For this approach to be successful with newspeople it must be resource-oriented. The success of the approach taken by EANE came from assuming a resource posture not an advocacy posture with the media. Pushing stories for the purpose of reaching a broadcaster's audience or a reporter's readership will compromise the effectiveness of the efforts made to build up trusting relationships. Max Ways called attention to this when he remonstrated against coercing people.

EANE rarely wrote about its own work. The story about the Association's research on Cape Cod was channeled throughout a regional ministerial organization. EANE concentrated on supplying reporters with information about the activities of other organizations. This is the meaning of "resourcing." The Association also provided spokesmen for more than one perspective on each issue it handled. This offered news people choices and presented a picture of diversity within the evangelical community. This invitation to newspeople to make choices also engenders openness and confidence.

## WHAT CAN WE LEARN FROM THE EANE EXPERIMENT?

The EANE experiment was intended for only a limited duration and lasted 18 months from inception to the conclusion of the program. It was an expensive enterprise, requiring fully a professional office, a support staff, mass mailing and computerized research capabilities and a network of both media contacts and resources.

It focused on a narrow area of endeavor and was not completely successful in all of its efforts, although at no time was any ill will expressed by media people toward the project.

The Evangelistic Association was able to marshall these resources because of its long-term presence in New England (over 100 years). The Association has no similar corresponding organizations in other regions of the country, so the model would be difficult to duplicate precisely elsewhere. But this does not mean that credible interdenominational media resource projects could not be developed in other regions. Such programs would, however, require far-sighted, careful financial backing to succeed.

There are also reasons why such an enterprise would not be likely to work with the "national media," as the Washington-based reporters like to call themselves. Local media are far more accountable to their audiences, even in major markets such as Boston, than are the Washington-based media because of the greater proximity of the audience to the writers and reporters in the local markets.

The problem on the national level is how to engender responsiveness. Confrontation and accusation do not generally produce cooperative and trusting relationships. This is as true for dealing with the "national" news media as it is for dealing with network programming executives or motion picture producers.

This does not mean there is no place for protest. Where there is gratuitous violence or promiscuous behavior on TV, letters of protest to broadcasters, to the corporate office of the program sponsor and to the regulatory agencies are in order. Where there is inaccurate or unfair reporting, a letter to the editor is in order. Organized activities such as the National Coalition on TV Violence, organized by Dr. Thomas Radecki, and the National Federation for Decency are also effective parts of the broader evangelical response.

## HOW CAN CHRISTIANS REVERSE THE TRENDS IN MEDIA?

But protest acts only as a brake on the decay. Reversing the trend calls for positive input. Christians must not only write to the editors; they must become editors. Christians must not only criticize the news reporters; they must become the news reporters. Christians should be buying and operating radio and TV stations, not to turn them into religious ghettos but to operate them as commercial enterprises. The same is true for newspapers.

Christians should enter the advertising business. That is one place where the real power of choice lies for influencing broadcasters. Christians should be flooding the creative arts and working as production assistants, engineers, producers and directors in film production companies. They should also invest in such companies.

This should not lead to just a proliferation of religious newspapers, advertising companies and production houses. Rather such groups should undertake to examine precisely the same issues which are not undertaken by others. Christians in advertising can sell Fords and Smith-Coronas and Tide as well as anyone else. Christians can report on the Senate, the Supreme Court and civil rights as well as anyone else. Christians can make TV sit-coms and miniseries and made-for-TV movies as well as anyone else.

In fact, it may be competition which breeds responsiveness in those institutions which prove unresponsive to other approaches. In Washington, D.C. a group of evangelicals organized by White House correspondent Forrest Boyd has inaugurated a national satellite radio news network. International Media Service (IMS) produces 114 hourly newscasts, daily and weekly news features, commentaries and analysis programs. IMS covers the White House, the House and Senate, the Supreme Court and international news from the Middle East, Central America and around the world. Over 100 United States radio stations carry the service, and it has proven so successful that United Press International has hired evangelicals to produce a similar service from IMS and its affiliates.

The force behind IMS's success is that it is not a religious news service. It reports on national defense, the federal budget deficit, environmental issues, scandals in the Legal Services Corporation and the entire spectrum of news. This includes relevant stories containing moral, ethical and religious dimensions.

In this case evangelicals have moved on to compete with the national media, and have been so successful that one of the nation's major news organizations has been forced to copy it. Indeed, here's a practical way to help influence our nation with Christian values. If none of your local radio stations purchase and air International Media Service programming, call and write urging them to do so.

## ARE YOU WILLING TO BECOME THE SOLUTION?

While there is ample evidence that a serious malaise grips both the journalistic and entertainment enterprise today, there is reason for hope. And this hope must be based on two key elements: prayer and Christian action in obedience to the will of God.

In the final analysis, the renewing movement of God's Holy Spirit will need to become the cleaning and purifying force in a society where He has been in times past. But as the Spirit leads, we must be willing to obey. And if we are not obedient to the voice of God, we cannot cast the first stone at the media.

The Apostle Paul asks the pertinent question, "Without someone to speak the truth in love, how will they hear?"

But we must earn the right to be heard. We must first listen, care and understand, and this is difficult. Since we, the Church, have held ourselves apart from the journalistic and creative communities for so long, we must humbly seek to learn of the world in which journalists and artists exist. We must be prepared for their just suspicions and skepticism.

And we must remember that it is not they who need our forgiveness but we who need theirs. We are the ones who abandoned them. It is true that they need the Father's forgiveness, but we need their forgiveness for being so unclear and so impatient for so long. Reconciliation can bring trust and productive relationships with the press.

---

## Study Questions

1. The author contends that the Church abandoned the media as early as the dawn of the motion picture industry, and that is in large measure the reason for the lack of spiritual values in the entertainment media today. Do you agree or disagree?

2. A network executive suggested to Chuck Colson that Christians should be expected to unconditionally tune in any "religious" programs the networks choose to air. Their failure to do so invalidates Christians' objections to current network TV programming. Agree or disagree?

3. The author argues that not only does the Church need to seek the forgiveness of those in the media who have been offended by the nature of their religious attacks, but the Church also needs to "earn the right to be heard." Agree or disagree?

4. There is a political axiom that says, "You should never chalk up to malice, behavior which can be more easily explained by ignorance." Does this apply to the Church's complaints about the behavior of the news media?

5. The author calls for Christians to enter the news media and the performing arts, both as owners and as employees. Do you believe God might be leading you to pursue a career in the media, despite the pressures which such a choice might involve?

**About the Author**

John Rodman is currently director of operations and programming at WXNE-TV, Channel 25 in Boston, Massachusetts. A 15-year veteran in radio and television, he has been a political reporter in Washington, D.C. for the International Media Service Radio Network as well as for various Boston radio stations. He has acted as a consultant for the Billy Graham New England Crusade and the Evangelistic Association of New England, and has written articles for *Christianity Today* and *The Boston Herald*. A frequent radio talk-show guest, John and his wife Laurel live in suburban Boston with their son Colin.

# 3

# ABORTION AND THE THIRD WAY OF THE KINGDOM

by
Norman B. Bendroth

In 1903, Harvard University had almost finished construction of a new building, Emerson Hall, to house its philosophy department. It was complete except for the inscription that would be posted on the marble mantel above the entrance. When asked by the university's president for suggestions, members of the department suggested Parmenaides' dictum, "Man is the measure of all things." But when they returned from their various watering holes after the summer vacation they found, much to their chagrin, that the president had carved instead the biblical question, "What is man that Thou art mindful of him?" (Ps. 8:4) on the marble facade.

## THE CONFLICT OF VIEWS
This story illustrates two competing ideologies at loggerheads. One view holds that man is autonomous and the center of human existence. The other affirms that God is the center and we understand ourselves only when, as

Calvin put it, we view "nature through the spectacles of Scripture."

Nowhere is the fundamental contradiction between these competing world views more apparent than in the abortion issue. In the words of the eminent British journalist, Malcolm Muggeridge, "Our Western way of life has come to a parting of the ways."

> Either we go on with the process of shaping our own destiny without any reference to any higher being than Man, deciding ourselves how many children shall be born, when and in what varieties, which lives are worth continuing and which should be put out, from whom spare parts—kidneys, hearts, genitals, brainboxes even—shall be taken and to whom allotted.
>
> Or we draw back, seeking to understand and fall in with our Creator's purpose for us rather than to pursue our own, in true humility praying, as the founder of our religion and our civilization taught us: Thy will be done . . . . [1]

Muggeridge thus penetrates to the heart of the abortion debate. The issue is not whether an unborn child is biologically human, but what value we attach to human life. Proponents of abortion have successfully defended the practice by emphasizing its social necessity; the debate rarely, if ever, focuses on the worth of a human being. Yet this is the question we must answer.

As we shall see, the humanity of the unborn child is not the fundamental problem. In the spring of 1981, a Senate subcommittee assembled a blue ribbon panel of scientists to address the question, "When does human life begin?" At issue was a piece of legislation designed to reverse the Supreme Court's 1973 *Roe* v. *Wade* decision legalizing abortion-on-demand. In a rare burst of intellectual humility, the Court had failed to arrive at its own conclusion on this question. In the words of Justice Harry Blackmun, "When those trained in respective disciplines of medicine, philosophy and theology are unable to arrive at any consensus, the judiciary, at this point in the development of man's knowledge, is not in a position to speculate as to the answer."[2]

The Senate panel had no such difficulty. Dr. Micheline Matthews-Roth of Harvard Medical School concluded that "it is scientifically correct to say that an individual human life begins at conception, when egg and sperm join to form the zygote."[3] Dr. Hymie Gordon, a geneticist at the Mayo Clinic, went so far to say that he had never read of "anyone who has argued that life did not begin at conception."[4]

But abortion advocates simply dismiss such scientific evidence as irrelevant. While not denying that the unborn are biologically human, they refuse to admit the moral implications of that fact. Some argue, as does Yale University Medical School Professor Leon Rosenberg, that scientific and medical evidence will never settle the abortion question. "Ask your conscience, your minister, your priest, your rabbi or even your God," he advises, "because it is in their domain that this matter resides."[5] Significantly, none of the panelists supporting permissive abortion directly refuted the testimony of their colleagues. To do so would be to "argue the inarguable," as Dr. Hymie Gordon put it.

Many advocates of abortion, however, do not believe that human life begins before birth. Others, while recognizing that abortion does take a human life, nevertheless defend its legality. An editorial appearing in the *New Republic* was unusually honest. "Those who believe a woman should be free to have an abortion must face the consequences of their beliefs," the writer pointed out.

"There clearly is no logical or moral distinction between a fetus and a young baby; free availability of abortion cannot be reasonably distinguished from euthanasia." Yet he concluded this blunt appraisal with the amazing insistence that "nevertheless, we are for it." In his view, the belief that human life must be sacred always was "too facile," and the "social cost" of preserving unwanted fetuses was "simply too great."[6]

In 1970, *California Medicine,* the official journal of the California Medical Association, published an editorial calling for liberalized abortion laws. The author, Malcolm Potts, admitted that "it has been necessary to separate the idea of abortion from the idea of killing, which continues to be socially abhorrent. The result has been a curious avoidance of the scientific fact, which everyone really knows, that human life begins at conception and is continuous whether intra- or extra-uterine until death."[7]

## A DISPUTE OVER VALUES

These two candid confessions lay bare the fundamental issue of the abortion debate. Neither the *New Republic* nor Dr. Potts denies the humanity of the unborn child; indeed, they affirm it. At issue is not biology, but the value we attach to humanity. The Senate subcommittee recognized this in its report, noting that those who "did not wish to accord intrinsic worth to the lives of unborn children" simply refused to call them "human beings."[8] Abortion is, therefore, not a debate over scientific facts, but a dispute over values. What is at issue is the simple fact that every abortion takes a human life.

### The Judeo-Christian Ethic

Let's return for a moment to our story of the Harvard philosophy department. In that episode, involving the choice of an appropriate inscription for Emerson Hall, we saw two world views butting heads. One claims that Man is the yardstick with which to measure the universe. The other places God at the center. In an ethical system recognizing that God alone orders the cosmos and defines Man's place and purpose in it, human beings have value at every stage of their development because they are members of His creation. This is the "sanctity of life" ethic, a primary Judeo-Christian belief.

## The New Ethic

In the other ethical system, human life is merely the product of chance, not design. Human beings have no intrinsic value; to be "meaningful," their lives must possess a certain quality. According to this "quality of life" ethic, therefore, some lives are simply not worth living.

This approach has become increasingly respectable, especially in academic circles. In the late 1960s and early 1970s, medical journals began to carry articles either advocating or applying the new ethic. Australian bioethicist Peter Singer, for example, announced that the Judeo-Christian "sanctity of life" ethic was obsolete. Writing in support of infanticide in the prestigious journal *Pediatrics,* Singer argued, "We can no longer base our ethics on the idea that human beings are a special form of creation, made in the image of God, singled out from all other animals, and alone possessing an immortal soul. Once the religious mumbo-jumbo has been stripped away," Singer wrote, " . . . we will not regard as sacrosanct the life of each and every member of our species."

Singer concludes with this frank observation: "If we can put aside the obsolete and erroneous notion of the sanctity of all human life, we may start to look at human life as it really is: at the quality of life that each human being has or can achieve."[9] For Singer, the humanity of the fetus is simply not "morally relevant."

## THE CONSEQUENCES OF *ROE* V. *WADE*

The first application of this new ethical standard was thrust upon the nation on January 22, 1973. On this day, the Supreme Court established a national policy of abortion-on-demand in its *Roe* v. *Wade* decision. In a 7-2 decision, the majority held that:

1. Until a human being is "viable" or "capable of meaningful human life" a state has no "compelling interest" in protecting the unborn child. For six months, or "usually" for seven months (the Court's reckoning) the fetus is denied the protection of law.

2. After the viability has been reached, the human being is not a person "in the whole sense," so that even after viability he or she is not protected by the Fourteenth Amendment's guarantee that life shall not be taken without due process of law. At this point he or she is, however, legally recognizable as "potential life."

3. A state may nonetheless not protect a viable human being by preventing an abortion undertaken to preserve the health of the mother (health being a medical judgment to be "exercised in the light of all factors—physical, emotional, familial and the woman's age—relevant to the well-being of the patient"). Therefore, a fetus of seven, eight or nine months is subordinated by the Court's reading of the Constitution to the demand for abortion predicated on health.

4. The Constitution also prohibits a state from requiring that the abortion be in a hospital licensed by the Joint Committee on Accreditation of Hospitals or indeed that it be in a hospital at all.[10]

### Historical Precedent Set Aside

The *Roe v. Wade* decision passed over two millennia of

moral, legal and religious testimony. And so the United States today has the most permissive abortion laws in the Western world. The Court rejected the strong legal tradition protecting the unborn. It dismissed the anti-abortion injunction of the Hippocratic oath—the paramount pre-Christian text on medical ethics—because it had gained universal acceptance only with the advent of Christianity. [11] Apparently, in the Court's view, an ethical norm, no matter how widely accepted, was irrelevant if it happened to accord with the Christian faith.

## Anti-abortion Laws Invalidated

The Court also invalidated the anti-abortion laws of all 50 states. And in so doing, it elevated "one theory of life" above all others, namely the "quality of life" ethic. The unborn did not enjoy the civil rights guaranteed by the Constitution for they were not "persons in the whole sense."[12] Human life, as a result, became a matter of definition rather than of fact. And the fetus was reduced to a cipher, a nonperson without any rights.

The 1973 ruling, in the view of dissenting Justice Byron White, enshrined the "quality of life" ethic, valuing the "convenience of the pregnant mother more than the continued existence and development of the life or potential life that she carries."[13]

## National Policy of Death Sanctioned

In having denied constitutional safeguards to the unborn child, our highest Court has sanctioned a national policy of death. Since its legalization in 1973, abortion has become the most common surgical procedure in the United States. The latest statistics show between 1.5 and 1.6 million abortions performed annually, more than 4,000 daily, one every 22 seconds. One in four pregnancies now end in abortion, and one in 10 women of reproductive age have had at least one abortion.[14]

## THE MESSAGE OF SCRIPTURE

The escalating practice of abortion and the quality-of-life world view which buttresses it are both contrary to the biblical Word. The Bible teaches the marvel of our creation and declares that we are made in God's image. To be image-bearers of the living God means that we possess a certain sanctity, a sacredness. We are unique among all other forms of creation, set aside "to glorify God and to enjoy Him forever," as the *Westminster Shorter Catechism* declares it.

### Deity

The message of the sanctity of human life is a bright thread in the tapestry of Scripture. Human dignity was established at creation when Yahweh fashioned Man in His own likeness. The creation narrative of Genesis teaches us that human beings are singled out from rocks and radishes and tapeworms—we are made in His image (Gen. 1:26-28). The *imago Dei* (image of God) is God's imprimatur, His declaration of our dignity. To be image-bearers means we are created to know God and to resemble Him, our Heavenly Father.

The inescapable conclusion of Genesis is that human beings are valuable because of who they are, not because of what they do. Each is endowed with an inviolable dignity on the basis of his or her creation.

### Dust

The Genesis account further teaches us that human beings are composed not only of deity, but also dust. The dust manifested itself in the Fall, a denial of the sanctity of human life. Sin's advent bent every dimension of our existence, including the way we view ourselves. Even before the giving of the Law, God established Himself as the Protector of human life. Within one generation of Adam's sin, Cain killed his brother. God's judgment was swift and direct (Gen. 4:6-14). Nevertheless, violence spread and provoked the judgment of the Genesis Flood (Gen. 6:11-17). After the Flood, God affirmed His commitment to life by commanding Noah and his family to punish those who shed innocent blood (Gen. 9:6) and by promising never again to destroy the earth by flood (Gen. 2:21; 9:15).

## Law

Out of the Creation ordinance of the dignity of human life flows the Law. The sixth commandment, "You shall not murder" (Exod. 20:13, *NIV*) is not merely a negative command, it is a positive injunction to respect all of human life. The ban on murder was repeated and intensified in the New Testament (Matt. 15:19; 19:17-18). When Jesus, as the new Moses, expounded the Law in the Sermon on the Mount (Matt. 5:21-24) He taught that murder is an issue of the heart. Any word or action that denigrates the dignity and humanity of any person is an offense against God whose image that person bears. New Testament writers also linked our obligation to love our neighbor with the concept of life: as love is the law of life, hatred is the law of death (1 John 3:14,15).

## Grace

God in His grace did not abandon the human race to its sin. In the face of Man's rebellion and violence, God came to us in Jesus Christ, restoring the sanctity of human life. Christ as Redeemer has done two things for His people. He first reinstalled us as God's children. The language of adoption is used to describe our new relationship to God (Rom. 8:14-17; Gal. 4:4-7). Secondly, Christ re-created us in God's image (Col. 3:30; Eph. 4:24). His image in us is like a mirror that is broken; still visible, but distorted.

In Christ, God's redemptive plan has come full circle. The human race was created to resemble its Maker and to know Him. But Adam's sin ruined that family likeness. With the introduction of sin, violence was born and quickly escalated between family members. Then Jesus Christ restored us to the original order established at Creation, re-creating us in God's image and calling us once again to resemble Him (Rom. 8:29). We are no longer illegitimate children, but God is now "our Father who art in heaven."[15]

## THE BEGINNING OF LIFE

The objection may be raised that this biblical-theological outline applies to adult human beings rather than nascent human life. The Word of God, however, speaks in loud, clear strains of God's active involvement with the unborn child. Perhaps the most eloquent option of Scripture describing God's heart toward developing life is Psalm 139.

David begins his Psalm by exclaiming over the all-pervading, ever-present, all-knowing God (vv. 1-12). He marvels in the knowledge that this God of grandeur understands him so intimately and even desires his presence. As he ponders these wondrous matters, David's thoughts return to the beginning of his own life. He begins v. 13 with the word "for," indicating he is about to arrive at a conclusion. God's present interest, the Psalmist reasons, necessarily grows out of His workmanship in the earliest moments of David's life within the womb (vv. 13-16).[16]

### God's Involvement

The Psalm teaches that God's intimate involvement with David predated his birth. God formed his "inward parts"—a reference to his internal organs—and "weaved" him in his mother's womb, a poetic account of what we now know to be scientifically accurate, for our skeletal structure is laced with layer upon layer of blood vessels, sinews and tissues. As David reflects upon this marvelous truth, he breaks into spontaneous praise, "I am fearfully and wonderfully made" (v. 14).

Truly, we are fearfully and wonderfully made. By the end of the first week of life, the new human being is a mass of different types of cells. By the end of the second week, these cells have become tissues. And by the end of the third week, organs have begun to form. In fact, human heartbeats have been detected as early as 18 days after conception. By six weeks, measurable brain waves are sending impulses throughout the body, causing its tiny developing muscles to kick. The embryo now has all the internal organs of a mature adult.

During the next four weeks, he will reach four inches in length. The baby grimaces, squints and frowns. He breathes amniotic fluid and will swallow more if the fluid is sweetened. He will stop swallowing if it is soured. After the sixteenth week, the baby will grow and develop at a rate that, if it continued throughout the remainder of pregnancy, the baby would weigh 14 tons at birth![17]

"How inspiring is the birth of a child!" observes commentator Edward J. Young. "The very wonder of the circumstances under which life is conceived and the embryo formed should produce fear within our hearts, for we are then in the presence of the Author of Life."[18]

David suggests in Psalm 139:15,16 that, even though the small, multi-celled embryo may not have been observable to the naked eye, God knew of its presence. God's eye was upon it in the active sense, superintending and cultivating the child's development. With the womb as His studio, the Master Artist created His work of art as He fashioned another human organism.

David understood himself to be a person in God's

hands throughout these verses. His constant use of the first person indicates that he understood God was dealing with him personally, not merely with the "products of conception" which would later become a person.

This phenomenon—that God's purposes are operative even before birth—is not uncommon in Scripture. Isaiah and Jeremiah were both called to their prophetic roles before their birthdays (Isa. 49:1; Jer. 1:5). John the Baptizer was filled with the Holy Spirit and set apart for service while yet in the womb (Luke 1:41-44). And the apostle Paul recognized that he was consecrated for his ministry to the Gentiles even as he was conceived (Gal. 1:15).

## God's Concern

God's concern for humankind extends to the point of identification with those He created. In the incarnation of Jesus Christ, God became a man like us in every way (Heb. 2:14-17). To be the perfect representative of humanity on the cross, Jesus had to experience all that it means to be human. Therefore, His life began at conception for that is when human life begins (John 1:1; Luke 1:26-35,41,42; 2:21).[19] Though the Son of God was humbled to clothe himself with human flesh, God was not ashamed to become a man. He ennobled human beings with His knowledge of them, His presence among them, His workmanship in them and His identification with them.

## THE SANCTITY OF HUMAN LIFE

Unquestionably, the sanctity of human life is at the core of Judeo-Christian teaching. The Bible cannot abide the destructive, violent nature of abortion, and neither has the historic Christian Church. The *Didache*, a second-century catechism written to instruct young converts in "the way of life" and "the way of death," forbade Christians to "slay a child by abortion."[20]

Christian antipathy toward abortion was well known in the ancient world. The second century moral philosopher Athenagoras appealed to that common knowledge when defending Christians against charges of cannibalism for eating "the body and blood" of Christ at the Eucharist.

How could we kill a man—we who say that women who take drugs to procure abortion are guilty of homicide and that they will have to answer to God for this abortion? One cannot at the same time believe that the fetus in the womb is a living being—as such in God's care—and kill one already brought forth into the light.[21]

Throughout church history, Christian opposition to abortion remained unequivocal. Commenting on Exodus 21:22f., the Reformer John Calvin wrote:

The fetus carried in the mother's womb is already a man; and it is quite unnatural that a life be destroyed of one who has not yet seen its enjoyment. For, it seems more unworthy that a man be killed in his home rather than in his field because for each man his home is his safest refuge. How much more abominable ought it to be considered to kill a fetus in the womb who has not yet been brought into the light.[22]

The modern church has continued in this heritage. Lutheran theologian and Christian martyr Dietrich Bonhoeffer stated frankly that the "destruction of the embryo in the mother's womb is a violation of the right to live which God has bestowed upon this nascent life."[23] "He who destroys germinating life kills a man," wrote Karl Barth in his *Church Dogmatics*.[24] "Two thousand years of Jewish-Christian history maintain," summarizes Harvard Professor of Divinity George H. Williams, "that the fetus is a person with the right to life." Clearly, those denominations and clergy that endorse abortion are beyond the pale of Christian history.

## THE ISSUE OF JUSTICE

As Scripture and Church history demonstrate, God has taken sides in this debate. That we Christians stand on the same side as well is critical. The abortion debate often focuses on the rights of individuals and, in a democratic society, this is entirely appropriate. The problem with this approach, however, is that it neglects the broader issues of justice for both individuals and society. In upholding the right to life of the fetus, some seem to express more concern for a multi-celled embryo than for a woman with an unwanted pregnancy and few options. But others parade the right of the individual woman to choose an abortion as a "fundamental" right, demonstrating little concern for the consequences of that decision.

### The Kingdom Ethic

The third way of the Kingdom of God balances the right to life of the fetus with the integrity and dignity of the pregnant woman. Pregnancy is not a tragedy. An unexpected child is not an adversary. Parents need not be the enemies of their posterity. The Kingdom ethic presents a better way.

Any ethic that is exclusively concerned with personal rights is deficient. Biblical ethics are in fact concerned with the applications of justice to our society. But justice is not simply fairness or right judgment. It is a redemptive word fully understood in the context of God's righteousness

(His "right-acting" character). Our redemption in Christ is expressed with the word "justice" when Paul writes that Christ's atonement demonstrates His "justice at the present time, so as to be just and the one who justifies the man who has faith in Jesus" (Rom. 3:26, *NIV*).

From this theological vantage point we see that justice embraces longsuffering and compassion as its qualities. "Justice is not retribution, but reconstruction . . . ," writes Mennonite theologian Myron S. Augsburger. "It is the active ministry of love. It is compassionate achievement of human rights with the ultimate sense of our being the truly human persons intended by our having been created in the image of God."[25] Biblical justice, therefore, must have as its goal redemption and renewal of persons in society by applying the righteousness of God.

## A Neighbor Love

The Righteous One calls Christians to be their "brothers' keepers" and to love their neighbors as themselves (Matt. 19:19; 22:37-40). What then is the best application of "neighbor love" to the problem of abortion? A Christian response, I would suggest, is two-fold: both political and pastoral.

## THE RESPONSE OF CHRISTIANS
### Political

The first aspect of a Christian solution to the abortion dilemma is political in nature. And, in our relationship to the State, two operating principles instruct us:

*1. The people of God have a moral obligation to the society in which they live.* Personal evils are corrected by personal repentance. But evil laws and public corruption are corrected by the law-making process and the formation of public policy. Often the Christian answer to a question of social policy will necessarily be political.

As the prophet Zechariah declared to the lawmakers and judges of his day: "Thus says the Lord of hosts, Render true judgments, show kindness and mercy each to his brother, do not oppress the widow, the fatherless, the sojourner, or the poor; and let none of your devise evil against his brother in your heart" (Zech. 7:9,10, *RSV*; see also Ezek. 45:9).

Christ Himself called His followers "the salt of the earth" and "the light of the world" (Matt. 5:13,14). He did not say that we will become like salt and light or that we should have the influence of salt or light, but that we *are* salt and light. Our obligation is to prevent rot in society and to make it more savory (morally acceptable), to shine light in darkness and to illuminate society with truth. Scripture speaks consistently of the social responsibility of all believers in Jesus as Saviour and Master.

2. *Christians are to protect and preserve the innocent and weak from oppression.* Our study of the scriptural view of the sanctity of human life confirms this (see Ps. 82:2-4; Deut. 27:25). Scripture teaches that silence in the face of violence merits God's special judgment, for we are culpable if we do not speak out. God commands us to:

> Deliver those who are being taken away to death,
> And those who are staggering to slaughter, O hold
> them back.
> If you say, "See, we did not know this,"
> Does He not consider it who weighs the hearts?
> And does He not know it who keeps your soul?
> And will He not render to man according to his
> work? (Prov. 24:11,12, *NASB*)

### Pastoral
The second aspect of a Christian solution to abortion then must be pastoral in nature. In every abortion there

are two victims: the unborn child and the pregnant woman. Indirectly, but undeniably, society-at-large is the third victim: abortion snuffs out the flower of our population at a rate of 1.5 million each year, dulls the conscience of our nation to accept death as an expedient solution to acute problems. It abandons the values of nurturing life and community to replace them with those of personal peace and affluence at any cost.

*The Unborn Child.* The first victim of abortion is the unborn child. In the early weeks of pregnancy, doctors perform abortions by inserting a sharp instrument of vacuum tube into the uterus through the cervix. The suction rips the child apart, sucking his remains into a jar. The majority of abortions are done in this manner.

The procedure most widely used during the second trimester of pregnancy (four to six months) is known as "dilation and evacuation." The abortionist dilates the woman's cervix and then uses forceps to clip apart the unborn child and remove the remains.

"Salting out" is another midterm abortion technique in which a salt solution is injected into the womb. The developing child is slowly poisoned and hours later delivered dead.[26] Evidence exists that the unborn child feels excruciating pain during this procedure.[27] Yet some children have survived such abortions and emerged alive. Even then, the baby is usually left to die.[28]

In the last trimester (seven to nine months), the child is surgically removed as in a caesarean section, but the umbilical cord is clamped off and the baby is left to die.

*The Pregnant Woman.* But the unborn child is not the only victim in an abortion. Behind the abstract abortion statistics stand countless individual women who experience the pain of crisis pregnancies. Many women are not given full and fair information regarding abortion. They are told it is a "safe legal" procedure with few negative consequences. But many find the experience to be just the opposite.

Nancy Jo Mann, founder of Women Exploited By Abortion, recalls, "The doctor said, 'a little fluid out, some fluid injected, severe cramps, then the fetus is expelled.' That isn't what it was. I felt my girl thrash around for an hour and a half 'til she died a slow death. I had hard labor for over 12 hours and delivered my daughter myself. She was beautiful—but dead at 5½ months."[29]

Neither are women told of the physical and psychological complications of abortion. The procedures can result in perforation of the uterus, a torn cervix, a variety of infections or hemorrhage. These in turn may lead to subsequent miscarriages, tubal pregnancies, sterility and even death.[30] Almost all women experience sleep disturbances, lack of sexual desire, depression, guilt or remorse, anger and mourning.[31] An abortion is frequently over in a matter of minutes; the guilt may last a lifetime. As the prophet Isaiah asked, "Can a woman forget her nursing child, and have no compassion on the son of her womb?" (Isa. 49:15, *NASB*).

## Historical

While others may forget and lack compassion, Christians cannot. Another generation of Christians in the United States provided a model for us in their response to a similar problem. During the revivals of the late nineteenth century, rescue homes for unwed mothers sprang up across the country. One such home was begun by Charles Nelson Crittenton, a millionaire whose world had collapsed when his daughter Florence died in 1882. His despair ended with his conversion to Christianity, and with characteristic zeal he threw himself into evangelistic and charitable work.

Once when Crittenton was exhorting two prostitutes

to forsake their way of life, he realized how hollow his words sounded, for he had no alternative to offer them— no food, money, or shelter. As a result, the first Florence Mission home for women opened in New York City on April 19, 1883. Soon overcrowded, the home received 176 girls its first year and averaged 250 annually.

In Atlanta, Mrs. Kate Waller Barrett, the wife of a clergyman, and Mrs. M.M. Wolfe established a rescue home after an abandoned woman appeared on Mrs. Barrett's doorstep one night. She realized how much the woman was like her, except for the men that she had loved.

These women hardly fit the stuffy, prissy stereotype of the Victorian woman. They met each situation with the love of Christ, always sensitive to the systemic evil, the poverty and indignity, that fostered individual sin. Mrs. Barrett of the Atlanta home viewed the women she encountered as "not fallen but knocked down," insisting that any intelligent person must "feel that society's attitudes toward the fallen woman is illogical, unjust and short-sighted." With unusual frankness in sexual matters, she and other Victorian reformers attacked the double standard that allowed irresponsible men to escape without condemnation and forced underpaid working women to choose between prostitution or slow starvation. Charles Crittenton described a factory which paid its women workers $1.50 per week. He reported, "About one-half of those girls were wrecked and their lives ruined by this system of wages."

Many of these "homes" achieved impressive results. In its first six years, the Florence Mission restored more than half of the women who entered its doors; the Door of Hope reported an 80% success rate. But what constitutes success? The standards were as high as the numbers of women restored. These missions viewed themselves as failures if the girl returned to sexual deviation of any kind, could not retain employment, or if conversion to Christ did not accompany her restitution. The ideal, as one report put it, was to enable girls to live "lives of happy usefulness."[32]

## Contemporary

This spirit of reform must burn in the hearts and minds of Christian believers today. To be savory, salty luminaries of the Kingdom in our day, we must heed the call of Micah "to do justice, to love kindness, and to walk humbly with your God" (Micah 6:8, *NASB*). The plaints of the needy in our bent society echo about us in the twentieth century no less than in centuries past.

Witness the anguish of one 15-year-old girl. In a letter brought to my attention several years back, this young woman told of her unintentional pregnancy. The pressures became unbearable as her parents refused to let her carry the child or see her boyfriend. The local Planned Parenthood counselor glibly informed her that her child would never be adopted. Her story is gripping.

> My abortion is something I wish I had never done. I can remember looking at the doctor when it was done and saw him putting my baby in a plastic trash bag and then throwing it away in a plastic trash bag. Do you know how that feels? . . . Have you ever lost something you loved dearly? I did, and I'm not proud of it . . . . If I had a place to go and people who cared about my baby and me, maybe my baby would be born and alive. It was supposed to be born this month . . . .
>
> You're hurting the girls that wanted their babies, but didn't have any alternative, but to have it aborted. But I want to say it hurts like "hell"

. . . . You people are against abortion, but are you willing to help young girls and women who don't have the money or a place to live? . . . Some of us women and girls are not killers. We're human too. And I can tell you having an abortion is killing me slowly . . . .

Ministries to women in situations like these are mushrooming across the country today. The Christian Action Council is on the leading edge of sponsoring ministries like this through its Crisis Pregnancy Center (CPC) program. A CPC is a locally organized and funded ministry which brings the resources of the local Church and the community to relieve the problems and pressures facing pregnant women. Each CPC offers free pregnancy testing; facts regarding pregnancy, abortion and alternatives; housing with Christian families for homeless clients; childbirth classes; clothing and furnishings to accommodate both mother and baby; classes for single parents; information on breast feeding and nutrition; referrals for adoption; medical care, legal assistance and other community services; and ongoing counseling and friendship. One such Center opened in November 1980 in Baltimore, Maryland with a part-time director, a handful of volunteers and a storefront office. In the early days, the Baltimore Center saw 260 women. Today, the Center has outgrown its facilities, is staffed with 60-plus trained volunteers, employs two full-time directors, and sees an average of 1,200 women each year.

Centers are finding that approximately 60% of the women who use the CPC services have a positive pregnancy test. Of these pregnant women, half usually are abortion-minded and half are undecided or want to carry their babies to term. After counseling with trained volunteers, however, some 80% of the pregnant clients decide to carry to term. Fully 60% of the women who had been abortion-minded changed their minds and chose life. Many are coming to Christ.[33]

## The Vehicle of God

This approach is the third way of the Kingdom which respects both the rights of the unborn child and the dignity of the mother. These two sets of obligations are not mutually exclusive, nor are they in competition with one another. The unborn child is neither an adversary nor an intruder. And pregnancy is not a disease to be cured. Both pregnancy and children are a gift from God. Consequently, the abortion problem will be overcome only as we act as a Christian community—not treating people as isolated individuals. Abortion is a two-sex, community affair involving the rights and welfare of women, fetuses, children, fathers, families and the rest of the human community.

The vehicle God will use to triumph over abortion and restore its victims is the Church. In a study of the prolife and prochoice movements, Sociologist John D. McCarthy has found that the success of the prolife movement, as with the civil rights movement, is due to the natural infrastructure of local churches. McCarthy's study also shows a deeper level of commitment among right-to-life people as compared to their prochoice counterparts who reveal religious apathy and who rely upon media campaigns and mass-mailing rather than upon churches to garner their support.[34]

To repeat, a Christian's response to the abortion problem in the United States should be two-fold: (a) We must actively seek to change the law which sanctions the destruction of nascent human life; and (b) we must provide life-giving ministries for women with stressful pregnancies.

But let us not be naive. On the one hand, some of my

more conservative friends suggest if we simply inscribe Judeo-Christian values into the Constitution once again, the problem will dry up and blow away. On the other hand, friends who are wary of the ability of the State to do anything effectively propose that the remedy is education, nurture and persuasion, rather than the coercive force of law. I would suggest that both positions are correct.

We need to influence our society from the top down and from the bottom up. The law is for the lawless (see 1 Tim. 1:9), and we must fiercely resist unjust laws. Yet there are also broken people whom we can assist long before the Supreme Court decision is reversed. People with prochoice/abortion convictions may be sincere, but they are sincerely wrong and need to be persuaded of the superiority of the Christian world and life view. This, too, is the third way of the Kingdom.

## The Life-style of Justice

The Christian who is not indifferent to the quality of life here on earth practices a life-style of justice that is necessarily lived in opposition to the prevailing values of our culture. Why? Because the Church is informed by a different view of reality: that what the world calls "miserable" God calls "blessed." We are members of the "upside down" Kingdom (see Acts 17:6).

Though Jesus was confronted daily by desperate human situations, not once did He solve a problem by eliminating the person or by suggesting that he or she should not have been born (read Matt. 5:14; 22:36-40; 25:37-40). Our Lord's mission was characterized by life (see John 14:6), and His desire is not that life merely be endured, but that it be lived in abundance (see John 10:10). His standards are much different than those of our culture; the primary right of life always takes precedence over creature comforts.

Therefore, a life-style of justice will be based on the *imitatio Christi*. Christ is the head, the Lord of the Christian, the Master, Teacher, Pathfinder and Example. A life-style of justice will mean loving our enemies in suffering service; identifying with the weak and oppressed; opposing individuals and institutions that violate the sanctity of human life; and serving as reconcilers and peacemakers (cf. Matt. 5:9; Jas. 3:17-18).

More than a decade and some 13 million unborn lives have transpired since the *Roe* v. *Wade* Supreme Court decision. At that time abortion was presented as a remedy for social problems, but where are the benefits? Parents of handicapped children still fend for themselves, unwed mothers are still ostracized, rape victims continue to be humiliated and the poor still struggle for simple justice and opportunity.

We must move toward creating a society in which material pursuits are not the end of our lives; where no child is neglected or hungry; where even defective children are regarded as valuable because they are made in the image of God and call forth our power to love and serve without reward. With this as our goal, then every child in spite of his or her capabilities or the circumstances of birth can be welcomed, loved and cared for; then every woman with a crisis pregnancy will be seen not as a "burden to society," but as a person in need of ministry and support.

As long as abortion is condoned, there is no justice and there can be no security, for God's anger is certain. With equal force, if Christians do not address the problems that lead to abortion or offer concrete, humane alternatives, they are perpetrating injustice. To think that a destructive medical technique is replacing love as the shaper of families in our society is very disturbing. A more candid confession of the exhaustion of compassion and social imagination could not be imagined.

Respect for human life should resonate deep within our hearts because it is in the heart of God. "Respect," wrote Karl Barth, "is man's astonishment, humility and awe at a fact in which he meets something superior—majesty, dignity, holiness, a mystery which compels him to withdraw and keep his distance, to handle it modestly, circumspectly and carefully . . . . In human life he meets something superior."[35]

Jesus said it best. "Whatsoever you did unto the least of these, my brethren, you did unto Me" (cf. Matt. 25:40).

---

## Study Questions

1. What does it mean to "bear the image of God"?

2. Imagine that a couple in your church expecting a child has undergone amniocentesis, a medical procedure which detects birth defects. The test is positive, indicating they may be carrying a defective child. Some people have advised them that an abortion is acceptable in this case because severely deformed or retarded children do not bear the image of God. In light of Genesis 1:26-28; Isaiah 45:9-10; and Exodus 3:10-12; 4:10-13; how would you advise them?

3. You have a friend who has come to you very despondent. She can only produce C+ work at the local community college even while trying her hardest, feels she can never please her boss and complains of feeling worthless because she has no special skills. How would you counsel your friend? Where should her value come from in light of this study? (See Ps. 139; Job 10:8-12; 33:4.)

4. "The wages of sin is death," the Apostle Paul wrote (Rom. 6:23). Why is it that every time we commit a sin we are not struck dead? Why is violence singled out as meriting God's special judgment which calls for death? (See also Exod. 20:13; Gen. 4:8-16; 9:6.)

5. The Bible teaches that Jesus Christ was made like us in every way to be the perfect representative of humanity on the cross (Heb. 2:17). What is the significance that He was conceived by the Holy Spirit? (See Luke 1:31; 41-44.)

6. Read Psalm 8. Note how it begins and ends. What things display God's majesty? What part do human beings play in God's plan? How does the creation order in Psalm 8 differ from modern thinking and practice?

## About the Author

Norman B. Bendroth is the Director of Communications for the Christian Action Council, the nation's largest Protestant prolife organization. He has the M.Div. (cum laude) from Trinity Evangelical Divinity School and the B.S. (cum laude) in Art Education from the University of New Hampshire. He has served on church staffs in New Hampshire and Illinois and is currently an elder at Washington Community Fellowship, an interdenominational church on Capitol Hill. He is also chairman of the board of the Capitol Hill Crisis Pregnancy Center. Norman is an avid Orioles's fan and enjoys cartooning, backpacking and guitar. He is married and his wife, Peggy, is a Ph.D. candidate in American Religious History.

# 4

# INTERNATIONAL RELIGIOUS LIBERTY AND THE GREAT COMMISSION

by
Kerry Ptacek

For Christians, religious liberty can be defined as simply the freedom to proclaim and to act on the gospel. It is not the same thing as the freedom from sin and death when Jesus is our Lord and Saviour. We can be free in Christ regardless of external conditions because no power on earth can separate us from this freedom.

As Paul said in his Letter to the Romans: "Who shall separate us from the love of Christ? Shall trouble or hardship or persecution or famine or nakedness or danger or sword?" Paul's answer, of course, was that "in all these things we are more than conquerors through him who loved us. For I am convinced that neither death nor life, neither angels nor demons, neither the present nor the future, nor any powers, neither height nor depth, nor anything else in all creation, will be able to separate us from the love of God that is in Christ Jesus our Lord" (Rom. 8:35-39, *NIV*).

But religious liberty is important. The gospel's demands on Christians require religious liberty. We are called to "go and make disciples of all nations, baptizing them in the name of the Father and of the Son and of the Holy Spirit" (see Matt. 28:19, *NIV*). These actions require freedom of religious speech (proselytizing), freedom to travel (mission) and freedom to administer the sacraments.

The freedom to proclaim the gospel does not exhaust a Christian's definition of religious liberty, for there must also be the freedom to act on the gospel. This is an essential component in the proper understanding of this question. There are many countries in the world that give Christians a great deal of freedom to worship and evangelize, but place restrictions against *acting* on the gospel.

Acting on the gospel can mean speaking out against what we understand to be a violation of God's laws. Such witness has been prophetic because of the prophets' criticisms of society and government. But whereas the prophets are speaking on God's behalf, Christians today act from their own interpretation of God's will as found in Scripture. And these interpretations have always led to disagreement. Perhaps this disagreement reflects the inability of any one person to know fully God's will.

As far as we can tell, the disagreements which flow from this aspect of religious liberty—the freedom to act on the demands of the gospel—can only be met in societies that are democratic. This does not mean that democracy is Christian, because democracy can err greatly from the Christian point of view. Democracy merely provides the possibility for Christians to both proclaim and act on the gospel.

This article surveys the state of international religious freedom. It is my assertion that countries of the world can be grouped into four general categories according to how much religious liberty exists. This survey will assist Christians in setting their priorities for seeking to expand the area of the earth where believers may proclaim and act on the gospel.

## TOTALITARIANISM

The basis of communist hostility towards religious liberty lies in its very nature, for it is a form of totalitarianism and a system which places all power—political, economic, social and cultural—in the hands of the state, usually through an agency of the totalitarian party. Totalitarianism is not really of the political Left or Right. Hitler's National Socialist regime, for example, was a type of totalitarianism, even though it is generally seen as extreme Right. No totalitarian regime can tolerate an independent center of power and loyalty—especially Christianity, which touches all the aspects of life that totalitarianism claims for its own.

In a communist regime, the state does not permit the Church to act on the gospel because that freedom represents a threat to the monopoly claimed by the ruling party. Church social-action programs are also prohibited because they are believed to undermine the government programs established to assure the dependence of the ruled. Exceptions are made when communist governments are in dire straits. But even then the government usually insists on state control of the "church" institution. Permission for churches in the United States to send relief supplies to Vietnam through supposed church bodies is an example of this pattern.

Some communist countries have sought to eliminate the very presence of Christian churches. Albania and North Korea are still using the most violent of methods toward this end, severely punishing any expression of Christianity. In Albania, Fatuci Shtjefen Kort, a secretly ordained minister, was executed for baptizing the child of a mother imprisoned in the same concentration camp with him. In Kampuchea, formerly Cambodia, Communists attempted to exterminate the small Christian community residing in that country.

After the 1917 Bolshevik revolution in Russia, Communists violently repressed the churches. Over 8,000 Orthodox priests, monks and nuns were killed in 1922 alone. Later, under Joseph Stalin, over 25,000 Baptist pastors were imprisoned; 22,000 of them died in the Gulag—the infamous Soviet slave labor camp system. The slaughter abated only when the Soviet government, facing defeat at the hands of their one-time ally National Socialist Germany, turned to the remnants of the Russian Orthodox Church for support in fighting what was then called "the Great Patriotic War." Some Protestant churches—including the registered Baptists—were brought into a similar arrangement during the 1950s in exchange for support of Soviet foreign policy objectives.

Communist countries—when they have given up the direct effort to completely extinguish Christian faith—have attempted to prevent Christians from evangelizing. Unable to uproot Christianity, Communists have fallen back on the hope that the number of the faithful would progressively decline. This policy has often extended to making it illegal for Christian parents to give religious instruction to their own children either in church or at home. For example, a young Soviet woman, Galina Vilchinskaya was among the more than 2,000 Evangelical Baptists arrested since 1961. Her crime: leading Bible study at a children's camp.

This relationship with the government often brings with it government secret police penetration and control of key church institutions. In 1980, a secret 1975 report by the Soviet government's Council on Religious Affairs to the Soviet Central Committee of the Communist Party surfaced in the West. The report, written by the deputy chairman of the council, V. Furov, makes clear the detailed control exercised over the Russian Orthodox Church by Soviet authorities.

According to Furov:

> The question of selection of [the Synod of the Russian Orthodox Church's] permanent members used to be, and still is, in the hands of the Council . . . the Council approves the final 'Decisions of the Holy Synod.'
>
> . . . appropriate officials of the Council conduct systematic work to educate and enlighten the members of the Synod, maintain confidential contacts with them, shape their patriotic views and attitudes, and exert necessary influence on the entire episcopate through the members of the Synod and with their help . . . .
>
> There is no consecration of a bishop, no transfer, without thorough investigation of the candidate by appropriate officials of the Council in close cooperation with the commissioner, local organs and corresponding interested organizations.

This system of control, with some exceptions, was exported to Eastern Europe with the advance of the Soviet army after World War II.

The establishment of Communist governments in Cuba, Vietnam, Laos, Ethiopia, Angola and Mozambique has led to an extension of the totalitarian pattern of church-state relations to Latin America, Southeast Asia and Africa. Ethiopia is still preoccupied with breaking the power of the churches. But the other communist governments have also implemented the "second stage" of secret police penetration of church institutions and manipulation of the churches' foreign relations—all for the benefit of the state.

Tragically, some Christians in the Free World have not understood that the presence of the Soviet-bloc Christians at international peace conferences and meetings of the World Council of Churches does not represent a genuine measure of freedom for these oppressed Christians, but rather represents the manipulation of the Church by its enemies. In spite of Russian Orthodox Church membership in the World Council of Churches since 1961, 10,000 Orthodox churches have been closed by the government in the last 20 years. Such a church is worse off than one which is repressed but left internally free. For instance, the Catholic Church of Poland has fought and suffered for its independence while the subverted churches decline. After his election as pope, John Paul II spoke from the spirit of that church saying: "Better a persecuted church than a compromised church."

## RELIGIOUS MONOPOLY: ISLAM

Some of Christianity's oldest churches, those of Syria and Iraq, are under virtual house arrest. When Christians sought to relieve famine in Somalia, they were expressly forbidden to mention that their Christian faith brought them to do such acts of mercy. In Egypt, Coptic Christians were the principal target of Arab socialism and today, under a more moderate government, are still subject to serious restrictions.[1] Nevertheless, Egypt and other countries with Moslem majorities—such as Indonesia, which permits Christian evangelism—suggest that Islamic countries are not necessarily inimical to religious liberty.

Islamic societies, unlike communist governments, do not seek to infiltrate and adapt the restricted Christian churches to monumental foreign policy objectives. Thus while Moslems, unlike Communists, may discriminate against Christians and make evangelism illegal, they do not violate the internal life and integrity of the Church.

How should we evaluate the "Islamic bloc"? Some would argue that the denial of religious liberty to other faiths is basic to Islam's sacred writings, the Koran. Jews and Christians are accorded a degree of tolerance as "Peoples of the Book," but are not to have the same religious rights as Moslems. In addition, the Koran forbids conversion from Islam.

It may be true that Islamic fundamentalism is not compatible with religious liberty. And in its most extreme form, Islamic fundamentalism is similar to totalitarianism. Indeed, some Islamic-socialist regimes such as Libya are one-party dictatorships strongly resembling National Socialism and allied with Communism. But most Islamic countries of the Middle East and North Africa are more comparable to the traditional form of religious persecution of one faith by another as found in countries such as Buddhist Nepal.

As recently as the early 1960s, several southern European and Latin American countries with Roman Catholic majorities have placed restrictions of varying degrees on the religious freedom of Protestants. This practice had once been a concern of the defenders of religious liberty but is now no more than a memory. Some governments still view Catholicism as the established church but this view has no more effect on the freedom of other Christians in those countries than does the establishment of Anglicanism in the United Kingdom or Lutheranism in the Scandinavian countries.

As we have seen, Communist and Islamic countries deny Christians the freedom to proclaim the gospel. These two rather general categories include all of Eastern Europe, most of mainland Asia—excluding only South Korea, Thailand, Malaysia, India and Israel—and northern Africa, almost half that continent's territory.

## AUTHORITARIANISM

The third category of countries, where there are religious freedom violations, is more acceptable than the Communist and Islamic blocs, yet still falls short of the Christian definition of religious liberty we introduced earlier. These governments permit a wide measure of religious liberty but at times prevent Christians from carrying out the demands of the gospel. Unlike the totalitarian system where independent sectors of society such as family, business and labor are infiltrated and subordinated to the state, some dictatorial regimes permit important sectors of society to remain relatively independent. For the sake of simplicity let us refer to these regimes as authoritarian.

Several of the countries that fall into the authoritarian category are also the scene of rapid church growth. South Korea, the country with the world's fastest growing Christian community, has arrested and imprisoned some Christians who, on the basis of their interpretation of the gospel, have sought to organize unions and community-action groups.

South Africa is another country which allows a relatively high degree of religious freedom and yet has restricted the political activities of Christians. Many believers who have felt impelled to criticize that country's system of racial segregation—apartheid—have suffered arrest or other restrictions on their freedom of action and expression.

Bishop Desmond Tutu, the general secretary of the South African Council of Churches, has been prevented at times from traveling overseas to anti-apartheid meetings. Others have been "banned," that is, they have had their political rights suspended. Still, the South African Council of Churches is free to obtain 95 percent of its budget from sources outside of South Africa, despite recent threats by the government to block this transfer of funds.

In times of civil strife, authoritarian countries which restrict the political activities of churches move from harassment and imprisonment to violence against churches and other critics of the government. Incidents of this nature have been reported in Guatemala, El Salvador, the Philippines and other authoritarian regimes.

Fortunately, authoritarian societies have the capacity of making the transition to democracy. In Europe we have seen Spain, Portugal and Greece shift to democracy when only a few years ago they were notoriously repressive. Argentina, one of Latin America's most violent countries, is now a democracy while El Salvador has continued the process of democratization in the face of left-wing guerrilla attempts to disrupt voting. Even recent Philippine elections hold promise for change.

Totalitarian regimes, on the other hand, have never made the transition to democracy and religious liberty except by way of military conquest, as in the cases of National Socialist Germany and the Caribbean island of Grenada. This is a very important difference between totalitarian and authoritarian regimes which is not appreciated by many critics of right-wing and military dictatorships.

As a result of the continual shift of authoritarian governments to democracy or to totalitarianism, it is difficult to give a clear view of the extent of an "authoritarian bloc." But, in a general way, we may say that such regimes are most prevalent in the non-Islamic and non-communist parts of Africa, Asia and Latin America.

## NICARAGUA: A SPECIAL CASE

There is considerable debate among Christians about the state of religious liberty under the newly established Sandinista government of Nicaragua. Some observers point to the seizure of evangelical and Pentecostal churches, the arrest or murder of Moravian Protestant pastors and lay leaders among the Indian population of the country's Atlantic coast, threats against the Roman Catholic bishops, censorship of the religious media, expulsion of foreign religious workers and missionaries, and government control of religious education. These observers have concluded that Nicaragua is merely a left-wing variant of the authoritarian pattern of restricting religious liberty.

This assessment seems to be upheld by accounts from United States church groups which have visited Nicaragua and found that pro-government religious groups are not repressed and are even encouraged. Some of these political pilgrims excuse Sandinista repression of certain churches, just as those of the opposite political persuasion can find excuses for repressing left-wing church activists in other countries. There is growing evidence, however, that Nicaragua is not merely a left-wing authoritarian regime—like Mexico, for example—but is moving toward communist totalitarianism.

The Sandinistas have sought to eliminate or subordinate all institutions independent of the Sandinista Front, the official ruling party. The remaining independent media, the newspaper *La Prensa* and the two privately owned radio stations must submit to prior censorship. Sometimes *La Prensa*, once the leading voice against the previous dictatorship of Anastasio Somoza, has had up to 90 percent of its contents rejected by the official government censor.

The totalitarian monument does not stop with the media, however. The two free trade union federations, which also opposed Somoza, are under constant pressure by the government to join the Front-controlled Sandinista Workers Center. Independent labor leaders have been harassed and arrested, union meeting broken up and legitimate strikes broken. The small, private enterprise sector that has not been taken over by the government is subject to complete state control. In effect, the business owners have been reduced to being unpaid managers of what is now government property.

The democratic parties which still exist in Nicaragua do not have the freedom to assemble or publicize their views and their leaders and offices have been repeatedly attacked by Sandinista mobs. These parties are threatened not only with being declared illegal but also with confiscation of their property by the ruling party and its leaders, if they do not participate in the controlled elections planned by the Sandinistas.

The Sandinista Front's control of everyday life extends into the neighborhood where the Sandinista Defense Committees administer the distribution of many rationed goods. These committees also operate as part of State Security, the political police. Modeled after the Cuban Committees for the Defense of the Revolution, each committee chairman is directly responsible to and employed by Security. The Sandinista Defense Committees are also used by the government for "spontaneous" demonstrations against critics of the regime.

Consider the following situations faced by the Nicaraguan churches. After the initial wave of repression against the Moravian Church, the Sandinista authorities did allow the church to reorganize. However, church, educational and health facilities were socialized and many church programs which had been the recipients of valuable foreign—often church—aid were subject to state control and supervision. And when the Moravians who had neither been imprisoned nor fled the country met in their denomination's General Assembly, the Sandinistas controlled the proceedings.[2] According to the respected liberal journal, *The Christian Century,* members of the political police sat among the delegates and told them how to vote on or amend resolutions placed before the body. And the first and last Assembly speakers were the top two military commanders of eastern Nicaragua—those responsible for seizing or burning many Moravian churches.

The situation in Nicaragua's other Protestant churches is no better but remains less blatant. According to Miguel Bolanos, a high-ranking defector from the Sandinista political police, the government is engaged in a concerted effort to recruit informers and place agents in the Protestant churches. The government has even placed agents in seminaries so that they may become pastors and move into key church positions. This is the beginning of exactly the same pattern of church manipulation reported in 1975 by V. Furov.

These events demonstrate that Nicaragua, while not completely totalitarian, is moving in that direction. Nicaragua is a country in transition. Therefore, the possible remedies are, for the time being, distinct from those countries still authoritarian or already totalitarian.

Nicaragua's Catholic bishops constitute the Sandinistas' main obstacle in the transition to totalitarianism and the subordination of the independent churches. The bishops have not only protested against attacks on Catholic schools, censorship of church media and seizure of Catholic churches. They have also used their strong base in the population to speak out in defense of other Christians as well as the independent press, free trade unions, democratic parties and private enterprise. The Sandinista drive for Communism may be crashing on the rock of the Nicaraguan Catholic Church.

Instead of expressing solidarity with oppressed Christians in Nicaragua, some Americans have chosen to side with the so-called "People's Church" which supports the Sandinistas. The "People's Church" in Nicaragua parallels the history of the "German Christians" who supported Hitler's National Socialist Revolution. The Christians in Germany who rejected the subordination of the church by the revolutionary state affirmed their resolve by declaring that only Jesus Christ is Lord. In other words, only Christ can make the total demands on our lives to which the totalitarian state aspires.

The case of Nicaragua is an important consideration for North American Christians. When Cuba went communist the repression of the churches was swift and unambiguous. Most Protestants fled the country, and a majority of the Catholic priests were expelled. In the 1970s, a current emerged among Latin American Christians which supported revolution and argued for an alliance between Christians and Communists. It was further contended that the failure of the Christian churches to actively support the revolutionary Left was the reason for their suppression in Cuba.

This notion remained untested in the western world until the Sandinista revolution in Nicaragua. The experiment of the Christian-Marxist alliance has yielded no variation in the communist pattern with this exception: the attack on the persecuted churches is now joined by persecutors who claim to be Christians. Before the attacks on evangelical and Pentecostal churches and seizure of their property by the Sandinista Defense Committees in the fall of 1982, much of the popular literature inciting these attacks had been produced by pro-Sandinista Christian organizations funded by the World Council of Churches and other church bodies.

## ACTION FOR INTERNATIONAL RELIGIOUS LIBERTY

Christians who wish to work for religious liberty in the world today must consider the different forms of religious persecution. They must also understand the three broad categories used to distinguish the violators of religious liberty: totalitarianism, Islamic and other religious monopolies and authoritarianism. There is also the special case of countries in transition, such as Nicaragua. For each category a distinct approach is necessary.

The most successful approach in totalitarian countries involves our speaking out publicly because persecuted Christians have repeatedly stated that their only protection comes from publicity. Therefore, we must recognize that the subverted churches cannot speak freely and must be spoken for. Today, what the totalitarian governments most desire from the United States is trade and technology. We should demand the price of religious liberty or offer no trade agreements or loans.

In the Middle East, only countries willing to make peace with Israel seem willing to permit some degree of religious liberty to Christians. This is sensible. Likewise, Israel is the Middle Eastern country with the greatest measure of religious liberty. Egypt should be the model for United States policy. Christians interested in eliminating religious persecution, therefore, should support United States efforts to convince its allies both to establish peace with Israel and grant freedom to religious minorities.

Christians can protect and promote religious liberty in authoritarian countries by supporting democracy. The restraints these countries place on religious liberties are identical to the limits imposed on political activity. Christians should press for democracy in these countries to free Christians to act on the demands of the gospel.

The situation in Nicaragua deserves extended discussion because it is a case where United States Christians have not only made the most serious of errors but where their corrective action can have the most positive results.

Although the leaders of the Front are professed Marxist-Leninists or communists, totalitarian state power has not been consolidated in Nicaragua. To prevent that outcome and to protect the future of religious liberty, Christians should support those institutions and groups in

Nicaragua struggling to preserve their independence from the state. This means that above all, Christians should express their solidarity with the Nicaraguan Roman Catholic bishops, for they remain the firmest protector of other independent sectors in Nicaraguan society.

The bishops' Easter pastoral letter, calling for dialogue between the Sandinistas and the anti-communist guerrillas, is especially promising. The anti-communist guerrillas, or "Contras," are twice as numerous as the leftist Salvadoran guerrillas. And unlike the Salvadoran guerrillas, the Contras have publicly offered to lay down their weapons, if permitted to participate in free elections. The bishops' call for dialogue offers the best chance for peace, reconciliation and democracy in Nicaragua.

Christians also must find ways to bring the plight of the Protestant churches in Nicaragua to the attention of North America and the world. These churches have been subject to far more political police infiltration and organized violence than the stronger Roman Catholic Church. Protestantism is most prevalent among those parts of the population most vulnerable to violence and abuse: the poor and the Indians in remote regions. Their story is rarely reported by the Managua-based foreign media.

One recent case illustrates how much suffering among Christians in Nicaragua may be going unnoticed and unprotested by the faithful in North America. According to the *New York Times,* a Pentecostal pastor, Prudencio de Jesus Baltodano, was tortured and left for dead by a unit of the Sandinista army simply because they discovered that he was an evangelical. A soldier cut Baltodano's ears off and slit his throat, just missing the jugular vein. The United Pentecostal Church International and the United States Surgeon General's office have extended assistance in the restoration of Baltodano's ears through plastic surgery.

But Baltodano and other sources have reported cases

of evangelicals who were not so fortunate. Baltodano tells of a pastor friend who died under torture, his nose cut off and other parts of his face mutilated.

Perhaps the saddest reason why Christians are not extending solidarity to their fellow Christians in Nicaragua lies in support extended to the Sandinistas by some United States churches. Nicaraguan tours have been organized by churches during which time only one side of the story is given, often by employees of various Nicaraguan institutions funded by United States churches, the National Council of Churches (NCC) and World Council churches. Some of these same churches have hosted speaking engagements throughout the United States for pro-Sandinista Christians.

This practice is similar to the NCC-sponsored tours for Soviet-bloc Christian delegations. In both cases, the fact that these spokesmen cannot safely deviate from the positions of their governments is ignored, and their comments attesting to religious liberty in their homelands are accepted at face value. It is important to note that since 1981, it has been illegal for Nicaraguans to criticize the Sandinistas while outside the country. This "crime" is punishable by a term of 3 to 10 years in prison.

Christians in churches which have supported pro-Sandinista religious groups in Nicaragua and hosted their leaders in the United States must be challenged to hear the other side. Beyond that, the leaders of these denominations—generally found in the National Council of Churches—must be told to stop funding organizations that justify the suppression of other Christians. These demands are particularly relevant for members of the United Methodist and Presbyterian churches, but a similar case could be made to the American Baptists, Disciples and United Church of Christ. We have even found some individuals and groups in the evangelical world following the mainline church pattern on Nicaragua.

In general, however, churches outside the mainline denominations also have sinned, but by omission, not by commission. While not lending support to the Sandinistas, neither have they extended solidarity to their victims. Southern Baptists, Pentecostals and other evangelicals should establish solidarity committees to protest Sandinista persecution and express their support for the initiatives of Nicaragua's Catholic bishops.

Religious liberty should be the matrix through which the international policy of the Christian churches is formed. To substitute other priorities—be they Left, Right or center—means relegating the Great Commission to an inferior position. But besides seeking the freedom to proclaim the gospel to the ends of the earth, we must demonstrate our love for our persecuted fellow Christians, so that the world will know that Christ is among us.

---

## Study Questions

1. What is the Christian motive for supporting international religious liberty?

2. What is the relationship between religious freedom and democracy?

3. What is the justification for the totalitarian hostility towards Christianity?

4. Is Islam incompatible with religious liberty?

5. What aspects of religious liberty are restricted by authoritarian regimes?

6. How does totalitarianism differ from authoritarianism?

7. Is there religious liberty in Nicaragua?

8. What kind of action is appropriate for international religious liberty by North American Christians when dealing with totalitarian, religious monopoly and authoritarian regimes?

9. How does the Nicaraguan case differ from the situations mentioned in question eight?

10. How have churches through their involvement made support for persecuted Nicaraguan Christians difficult?

## Suggested Readings

The Institute on Religion and Democracy (IRD) was established in the Spring of 1981 to strengthen the link between Christian faith and democratic values in our churches. The IRD can provide publications and speakers on international religious liberty. Titles of special interest include:

"Christianity and Democracy," a statement by the IRD.

"Nicaragua: Revolution Against the Church?" Kerry Ptacek

"The Catholic Church in El Salvador," Kerry Ptacek

"Must Walls Confuse?" George Weigel (a critique of the study on churches in Eastern Europe)

"The Captive Churches and the Ecumenical Movement," J.A. Hebly.

"Grenada: Archive of Church Subversion." Interview with Michael Ledeen with a reproduction of a captured document on Marxist strategy toward churches in Grenada.

## About the Author

Kerry Ptacek is director of research for the Institute on Religion and Democracy in Washington, D.C. Before joining the IRD, Mr. Ptacek worked as education director of Frontlash, a youth program of the AFL-CIO. He is a graduate of the University of Michigan and an active Presbyterian layman.

# 5

# THE CHRISTIAN AND THE PROBLEM OF CRIME
## What We Can Do About It
by
Daniel W. Van Ness

It was late afternoon one day in November when I received a telephone call from the woman who lived below us in our two-flat apartment building.

"I just got home," she said. "Our apartments have been broken into. You had better come."

The burglars had been there sometime in the early afternoon. They had rung both doorbells to make sure no one was home, them jimmied the front door of the building. Both apartments were unlocked, but our door had a catch in it which apparently led the burglars to believe it was locked. They kicked the door in, destroying the jamb.

They had ransacked both apartments. Drawers were pulled out and their contents disturbed; closet doors stood open with clothes pushed around. Our brand new clock-radio was gone, as was a camera, an old watch and a beautiful alarm clock my wife had purchased on a trip to Switzerland. The people downstairs were missing similar valuables. Apparently the intruders had taken only small items they could hide easily.

The police arrived more than an hour after we called them. They didn't bother to come upstairs to see our door or apartment; they just filled out a report so we could file insurance claims. They said it was unlikely the burglars would be caught and, warning us that they might come back for larger items, suggested we install better locks. They also recommended that we move to a safer neighborhood.

We slept two nights with a door that would not lock. We came home each day apprehensive that the "return visit" the police had predicted might have happened already. I spent a day and a half repairing our door. We never filed an insurance claim for fear that the raised premiums would be too expensive.

Our experience was not unique. According to the United States Census Bureau, one out of four households experienced some kind of crime last year. While this is a decrease over previous years, it suggests that victimization and fear are pervasive in this country. One public opinion survey, for example, found that half of the American people were afraid to walk the streets within one mile of their houses.

As a result, crime becomes not only a public policy issue, but also a political one. Law and order speeches have become a basic part of American political life. Of course, no one would argue against law or order. But the criminal justice system can become the fall guy in the political process. As elections approach, the temptation is to "talk tough" about crime. This translates into longer prison sentences, mandatory imprisonment laws and the like. The dilemma of what to do about crime is made painfully real by the stories of those caught in crime as well as victimized by it.

## A TRUE STORY

The 18-year-old stood before the judge for sentencing. He was part of a ring of boys his age who had burglarized houses all over town. They had stolen an estimated $150,000 worth of goods.

The judge faced considerable community pressure to do something forceful, to send a message to high school students that crime does not pay. The victims were frustrated, angry and resentful. Police had discovered that the teenagers were committing the crimes because they wanted to buy cars and maintain a high standard of living. It was easier and faster to break into people's houses than it was to get a job.

What should the judge do? How should Christians respond? Ought we to agree with the law-and-order rhetoric? Does Scripture have something to say about how our criminal justice system could become more equitable and effective?

## A REVIEW OF THE ISSUES

Let's first review some crime-related issues that are being debated today and then consider a biblical framework with which to examine these issues. After that we will return to the rest of this story and what the judge decided.

### Issue 1: Crime Rates

During the 1970s, the number of crimes reported to the police increased dramatically. The FBI compiles these statistics into one of two major indexes of criminal activity in the United States. The other index is the Census Bureau survey conducted every six months which determines how many households have experienced a crime during the past half year. Interestingly, the Census Bureau index did not show an increase during the 1970s, but did reveal that a staggering one out of three households were affected by crime each year. This figure remained constant throughout the decade.

Perhaps the best explanation for the difference between the two is that while crime remained basically constant during the 1970s, more victims of those crimes began reporting those incidents to the police. Since crime reported to the police is what the FBI tabulates, its figures may have simply reflected an increasingly complete view of the extent of crime, rather than indicating that crime was rising.

In any event, the 1980s have produced a dramatic drop in both reports. The 1981 FBI statistics showed no increase in crime; in 1982, a 3 percent decrease; and in 1983, a 7 percent decrease, the biggest drop since 1960.

And the Census Bureau study agreed. Their 1983 survey showed a decline in victimization to one out of every four households.

Several explanations have been given for this phenomenon. For one thing, the number of people in the 15-25 age group is declining. These appear to be the "crime prone" years, and a smaller population within that age-group means less crime. If this is true, then the drop in crime is likely to continue throughout the 1980s.

Another plausible explanation is that neighborhood crime-watch programs are working. Studies have shown that crime goes down in neighborhoods with such programs (and up in the surrounding neighborhoods).

## Issue 2: Victim's Rights

Crime involves four parties: the victim, the offender, the surrounding community and the state. But the criminal justice process focuses on only two of the parties: the offender and the state (e.g., *State of Illinois versus John Smith*).

This was not always the case. In the Old Testament, all four parties were involved in fixing responsibility for a criminal act and in bringing restoration to the victim. For example, thieves and other property offenders were required to pay restitution to the victim. The community was to help the offender and victim work out a fair payment. If they had difficulty in doing this, the case was taken to priests or judges for final determination.

Over time, however, the state's role increased, in part to curb vigilante justice, but also to facilitate the growing powers of centralized government. The result was that increasingly the victim was excluded from the criminal justice process. As the state became more powerful, protections were established to protect defendants from arbitrary or unfairly intrusive government actions in investigations and prosecutions.

Growth of the victim assistance movement has resulted in increased public and private resources to help victims deal with the impact of crime. It has also produced a variety of recommendations for reforming the criminal justice process. Many proposals are excellent and much-needed. Others, however, have nothing to do with victims. Instead they restrict the defendants' rights or mandate long prison sentences. Such measures should be discussed on their own merits. The true value of "victim's-rights" proposals should be gauged by asking how the reform will benefit *victims*.

## Issue 3: The Purpose of Prisons

The use of prisons to punish offenders is a uniquely American innovation. In 1790, Philadelphia converted its jail from a place to hold defendants prior to trial, to a place of penitence—a penitentiary—for those convicted of crimes. The offender was placed in solitary confinement and given a Bible and regular visits by the warden and a minister. The reformers hoped that offenders would be rehabilitated when they were separated from bad moral influences and given biblical training.

However, there were problems from the outset. Many early "penitents," locked in their solitary cells, went mad, and there was little evidence that this treatment produced rehabilitation. But the idea had caught on, and by the 1850s all states had adopted imprisonment to punish crimes.

Four reasons have been given to justify imprisonment to offenders:

- Incapacitation. A person locked up in prison cannot commit new crimes outside of prison.
- Deterrence. The knowledge that criminals are punished will keep potential criminals from breaking the law.
- Rehabilitation. Services can be provided to rehabilitate the offender.
- Punishment. Society must provide sanctions to be used against those who violate the law.

The one function unique to prisons is *incapacitation*. Prison provides a place where dangerous offenders can be physically restrained from committing new crimes in society. It is interesting to note, however, that only about half of the nation's prisoners are convicted of violent offenses. The other purposes can be served as well or better through other, less costly sanctions.

First, law enforcement experts generally agree that what deters people from committing a crime is the expectation of being caught and punished, not the severity of the punishment. This is why drivers do not speed when they see a police car behind them; they know they will be pulled over.

Since only one crime out of ten results in a conviction, the deterrent value of *any* punishment is slim. Increasing the potential punishment will do less to deter crime than increasing the likelihood that the offender will be apprehended. This is why neighborhood crime watch programs have been successful. Criminals know they are more likely to be caught in these neighborhoods.

Second, few criminal justice professionals believe that prison rehabilitates. Norman Carlson, director of the Federal Bureau of Prisons, has said, "I've given up hope for rehabilitation, because there's nothing we can do to force change on offenders. Change has got to come from the heart." To put an offender in prison with other criminal offenders, hoping he leaves the abnormal society of the prison a healthy and law-abiding person, is a curious strategy. Far too often the opposite occurs, and the offender is released a potentially more dangerous person than when he went to prison.

Third and finally, prison's purpose is punishment. Punishment, in the scriptural view, serves justice. Those who violate the law must face an appropriate sanction, or else law becomes simply an expression of hoped-for behavior.

In the United States, prison and punishment have become almost synonymous. But this is a recent development. Until 200 years ago, prisons were used only to hold people prior to trial or punishment. Genesis tells us that Joseph was thrown into prison. But as we know from what happened to his fellow prisoners, the baker and the cupbearer, that prison was used to hold people until they were tried or punished. And there were a whole array of punishments.

The predominant punishment in the Old Testament was restitution. The offender was required to repay the victim according to a formula set down in the Law. Zacchaeus refers to this in the New Testament when he comes down from the sycamore tree and has lunch with Jesus. He promises to pay back four-fold anyone that he has defrauded in his tax collection. That was what Jewish law required.

There were even provisions in the Old Testament to cover situations where the offender had no money to repay the victim. The offender had to work off the debt by performing free service for the victim.

So while the particular punishment of prison serves several purposes, other punishments do as well. The unique role of prisons is to incapacitate violent and dangerous offenders.

## Issue 4: Prison Overcrowding

America's prison population is growing dramatically. The number of prisoners has more than doubled in the last decade, going from 200,000 in 1973 to 438,000 at the end of 1983. What do these figures mean? Simply that our prison population is now growing 15 times faster than the general population.

We use prisons more than any country in the world, other than South Africa and the Soviet Union. In fact, our prison population itself is now larger than the population of 20 member countries of the United Nations, larger than Alaska and Wyoming, and roughly the size of Atlanta and Pittsburgh.

With such explosive growth, state and federal officials have been struggling to find room for all the prisoners. Virtually every state has exceeded its prison capacity. In 18 of these states, prisoners are sleeping on the floor. In several, chapels have been converted into dormitories to hold the overflow.

Thirty states are under court order. Conditions in one or more of their prisons are so bad, a judge has ruled that it is actually "cruel and unusual punishment" to send someone there. Why? Because of the marked increase in violence, disease, suicide, disciplinary violations and deaths that result from overcrowding.

Overcrowding affects the general public as well. Attorney General William French Smith's Task Force on Violent Crime stated in its 1981 report that overcrowding was the number one problem facing corrections authorities. It found a substantial number of cases where serious offenders who should have been incarcerated received probation because there was no prison space.

A simple answer to prison overcrowding is to build more prisons. But states are discovering they cannot build their way out of this crisis. Prisons are just too expensive.

States spend an average of $60,000 to $80,000 *per bed* to construct a typical prison. That's just under the median cost of a new home in the United States. And construction costs are only the beginning. A prison will cost 12.5 times more to run for 30 years than to build. This means that a prison costing $80,000 per bed to build will cost an additional $1,000,000 per bed to run over the next 30 years!

It takes an average of $15,800 to keep one person in prison for a year. That cost is more than room, board and tuition charges for a year at Harvard or Yale.

In other words, prison overcrowding has become an economic as well as a criminal justice issue, one that the courts are requiring public officials to resolve.

### Issue 5: Sentencing Innovations

Faced with the prohibitive cost of building new prisons and the realization that for some offenders other punishments may be more useful in serving the purposes of the criminal justice system, many states have begun to implement alternative punishments.

In most states, the correction authorities have begun by identifying the nondangerous offenders who are being sent to prison. These offenders are then either diverted to other forms of punishment or released from prison early and placed under intensive parole supervision.

For example, a number of states have established restitution and community service programs for property offenders. These offenders are required to repay their victims and to perform free work for a charity or a government agency in their community. In properly run programs the success rate is high, because the offender knows that, if he fails to perform adequately, the judge will order him to serve the rest of his time in prison.

Georgia, Texas, and several other states have supplemented this program with intensive probation. An offender subjected to intensive probation is required to set a daily schedule with his probation officers. One officer makes three surprise visits throughout the week to make sure the probationer is keeping to his schedule. The other officer meets with him twice a week for counseling and other assistance.

These states have discovered that they can enforce appropriate behavior at a fraction of the cost of prison. Georgia has saved $5.4 million per year; Texas saved $8 million last year. And repeat offender rates are lower. Alabama has experienced a recidivism rate of only 17-18 percent for people in intensive probation compared with a 25 percent rate overall.

Other states have released prisoners early to alleviate overcrowding. Last year over 24,000 inmates nationwide had sentences shortened to make room for new inmates. Some states used a formula to identify those least likely to commit a new crime. In others the legislature has reduced all sentences by 60- to 90-day intervals.

As would be expected, some of these released prisoners have committed new crimes, a few of which have received a great deal of publicity. But overall the recidivism rates for people released early has been about the same as for those serving their full sentences.

## A FRAMEWORK FOR DISCUSSION OF THESE ISSUES

While we must consider economics as we evaluate our criminal justice system, no one wants to settle for a second-rate criminal justice system simply because that's all we can afford. Fortunately, we have alternatives.

The Old Testament justice system was built on *restitution*. The advantage of such an approach is that it blends two ideas; we must hold an offender *responsible* for his conduct, and we must do so in a way that promotes *restoration* of the victim.

*Responsibility* is a major theme in Judeo-Christian thought. Individuals are responsible for their own acts and therefore are obligated to accept the punishments that result.

But *restoration* is an equally important concept which should help shape the form of that punishment. The offender must not only accept responsibility for his acts, he must also be required to take appropriate steps to restore the victim.

Such an approach answers the concerns being voiced by many victims today. Instead of being excluded from the criminal justice process, a restitution-based approach recognizes and enforces the most fundamental right of the victim: the right to be made whole.

Although violent and serious offenders—that 50 percent who pose an ongoing danger to society—must be locked up for our protection, the other 50 percent of the prison population could be punished in ways, such as intensive supervision coupled with restitution and community service, that promote restoration of the victim. This would have the additional benefit of lowering the prison population and avoiding costly prison expansion.

Restitution-based reform would require three changes:

1. Create a variety of criminal punishments for judges to use, including restitution and community service.

2. Reserve imprisonment for dangerous offenders who must be incapacitated.

3. Punish the other offenders—the non-dangerous ones—in ways that require them to accept responsibility for restoring the victim. Courts around the country are using this approach with success.

## THE REST OF THE STORY

What happened to our teenage burglar, introduced at the beginning of this article? In his case, the judge concluded that the defendant was not likely to ever burglarize houses again. "You have been caught," he said. "I think you will find it easier and safer to work for your income rather than steal it. But you broke the law, and I must see that you face the consequences. So I am sentencing you to do three things. First of all, I order you to perform community service."

And every Saturday (since he was still going to school), the young man did free work for the city. He painted buildings and cleaned up the park and that sort of thing. It was conspicuous punishment.

"Second, I order you to pay restitution to the victims." This meant repaying the market value of the items stolen. That amounted to much more than what the teenager got when he fenced the goods.

The judge gave him time to get a job and then took most of his paycheck for restitution payments. And because the judge wanted the defendant to know what it is like to be burglarized until he had lost everything he owned, part of the restitution order was to sell all of his property and put the proceeds into the restitution fund.

Initially the young man thought that meant only his car, which he had purchased with the proceeds of the crime. And it did mean his car, but it also meant *everything* else he owned, except for his clothes and his bed. It even meant the trophy he had won at a track meet. It meant his baseball bat. He had to sell everything that he owned so he would understand that, to their owner, personal belongings have a value greater than their monetary worth.

"Third, the victims want to talk to you about the crime. They have questions they want to ask you and things they want to tell you. So I want you to sit down and talk to them about it."

As it turned out, that was the toughest part of the sentence. The defendant said later that he would rather have done almost anything else. But he met with them.

The victims were very angry. They had been collectors of antique oriental furniture for years. So what they lost in the burglary was very valuable. But the couple had lost more than valuable furniture and art. They had lost memories. Their custom had been to purchase the antiques as souvenirs of trips and other memorable events. For example, one of the stolen items was a Ming vase they had purchased 10 years earlier at the end of a month-long vacation in Europe.

"Do you understand what you took from us?" they asked. "It was more than a beautiful, expensive vase. It was a memento of our trip. When guests admired it, we could talk to them not only about the vase, but also about our trip to Europe."

The young man was genuinely remorseful. He was beginning to understand what it was like to be victimized and to experience loss. And he wanted to make it up to them. The couple proposed a fascinating idea.

They told him that as a down payment on his restitution he should go to an antique store and find something he thought they would like. If they agreed, then he would buy it.

So he went to several stores and finally found a beautiful oriental coffee table painted with black lacquer with a delicate flower design. He was giving them something that fit them as individuals, and they received something from him that showed he was a sensitive young man, not simply a burglar.

Although the couple lost one memento, they gained another. Now when visitors put down their coffee cups and comment on the beautiful table, one of them says, "There is an interesting story about this coffee table . . . . "

## STRATEGY FOR ACTION

The judge in this story was able to impose a restitution-based sentence. His decision benefitted the victims, saved the state thousands of dollars, and held the defendant responsible without subjecting him to the violence, idleness and destructive influences of an overcrowded prison.

It is easy to see how judges, legislators and other public officials can bring about reform. But what can private citizens do? Can an average Christian really help accomplish change in the criminal justice system?

The answer is *yes*. Right now around the country people like you are taking effective steps to accomplish reform. The most successful ones follow a plan of action.

### First: Get the Facts

You now know more about the criminal justice system than most people. But do a little more investigating.

Are the prisons in your state overcrowded? What would it cost to build new ones? How many of your state's prisoners are nonviolent offenders who could be punished through restitution or community service instead? Are these programs available in your state?

The best way to get this information is to contact your state corrections department or your state legislators. But reform organizations can also help you. Just about every state has a local group working on reform, or you can contact a national organization like Justice Fellowship which monitors what is happening in each state.

Collecting this information is only part of the process. There are several ways you can get first-hand knowledge of how the criminal justice system works.

Visit a nearby prison. As a taxpayer you have the right to see what is happening with your money. Prisons do have security reasons for screening visitors, so call ahead to ask how you can tour the facility.

Get involved with a prison ministry. This will help you understand more about the kinds of people who are in prison, and will give you an opportunity to serve.

Sit in a courtroom for an afternoon and watch how cases are handled.

Talk to the police about crime prevention programs that are working in your state.

### Second: Know the Arguments for Reform

Review the issues and the framework for solutions discussed earlier in this chapter. How do these fit with what you have learned about your state? What would be the most compelling argument you could make to your friends for criminal justice reform?

Often the cost of imprisonment gets people's attention. How much does it cost to keep a prisoner for a year compared to a year at your state university?

Follow up by thinking about and discussing the principles of responsibility, restoration and restitution.

### Third: Let Other People Know What You Have Found

Everyone has a group of people he or she influences. Who are the people who pay attention to your ideas? They probably have not thought much about these issues, and they will be curious about what you are learning. Let them know what you have found and ask them to help.

Although most people do not think so, you can have a real influence on state and federal representatives. These people do read their mail, and most of them get very little about criminal justice. A brief, polite letter explaining your view that nonviolent, nondangerous offenders should be punished through restitution and community service will be effective.

### Fourth: Find Other People to Work With

It is much easier to work on a project like this with other people. Have a friend help you lead a discussion on criminal justice in a Bible study at church. Find out whether your denomination has a staff person or committee working on criminal justice issues.

Ask your state legislators to suggest a local reform organization working for these changes. Contact national organizations as well. Justice Fellowship, for example, helps people around the country work for reform and provides materials, ideas and information on helpful steps being taken around the country.

### Fifth: Be Specific

Identify for the people you are working with the specific changes that need to be made in the criminal justice and punishment system in your state. These should not be trivial changes. There should be some possibility for change and success. There may be legislation that should be supported or a new report that should get attention. Be ready to make specific recommendations when people ask what should be done.

If you know what you want done, do your research and let people know. Change will happen. It did in Indiana. In that state, Justice Fellowship worked with a group of Christians who were concerned about the problems in the state's criminal justice system. They first checked with state officials and discovered that Indiana was under court order to improve its prisons. The state was considering a $200 million prison construction program to ease over-crowding, even though officials felt there were a substantial number of prisoners who would pose no danger to society if they were punished outside of prison.

Their next action was to form a task force to raise support in the Christian community for reform. They agreed on those arguments that would best aid passage of a bill to set up local restitution and community service programs.

This group of dedicated believers also spoke in churches, civic clubs, professional meetings and on radio shows. They wrote letters to friends and business associates. They identified hundreds of people who agreed on the need for change. And ultimately they succeeded.

As a result of their activities and those of other concerned people throughout the state, Indiana's legislature appropriated $2.8 million to develop those local programs. (A subsequent study found that for every dollar spent in this way, the state saved $23.)

The hard work and perseverance of committed Christians paid off. And they found out that other people were also ready to support changes that were appropriate.

Yes, Christians can be salt and light, even in the criminal justice system. If enough of us work together, we can see similar change take place in every state.

## Study Questions

1. In the beginning of civilized society, how was crime and punishment viewed? In 1984, how is crime and punishment viewed? Are the two views different? In what way? Why?

2. What does the Old Testament advise about crime and punishment? The New Testament?

3. What is a violent and a nonviolent offender?

4. What do prisons do best?

5. Give an example of restitutionary punishment? Who might most appropriately qualify for this form of punishment?

## Suggested Readings

American Friends Service Committee, *Struggle for Justice*. New York: Hill and Wang, 1971.

Colson, Charles *et al.*, *Crime and the Responsible Community*. Grand Rapids: Wm. B. Eerdmans Publishing Co., 1981.

Lewis, C.C., "The Humanitarian Theory of Punishment," in *God in the Dock*. Grand Rapids: Wm. B. Eerdmans Publishing Co., 1970.

McHugh, Gerald A., *Christian Faith and Criminal Justice*. Ramsey, N.J.: Paulist Press, 1978.

Mitford, Jessica. *Kind and Unusual Punishment: The Prison Business*. New York: Random House, Inc., 1974.

**About the Author**

Daniel W. Van Ness is Vice-President of Justice Fellowship, a Washington, D.C., organization formed by Charles W. Colson and Prison Fellowship to promote criminal justice reforms. Mr. Van Ness has conducted extensive state and federal lobbying on this issue, as well as public education campaigns. Prior to working with Justice Fellowship he practiced law in Chicago for six years.

# 6

# THE PORNOGRAPHY REVOLUTION
## Is Pornography Only Dirty Pictures?
by
March Bell

Pornography is not just dirty pictures. It is cultural totalism. In the words of Irving Kristol:

> Obscenity is not merely about sex, any more than science fiction is about science. Science fiction, as every student of the genre knows, is a peculiar vision of power: what it is really about is politics. And obscenity is a peculiar vision of humanity: what it is really about is ethics and metaphysics.

The truly dangerous pornography in our culture is not the debasing garbage sold in brown wrappers at the back of a pool hall. As Rousas Rushdoony has pointed out, "The pornography factories still turn out the old garbage, but now with a difference: it has become *garbahzh,* pretentious garbage masquerading as the new enlightenment and new freedom."

As these quotes suggest, there is much more to pornography than explicit visual depictions. Obscenity is only one aspect of an ethical and social revolution.

## THE LURE OF DECADENCE

Evidence shows that the popular and least offensive pornography has been the most effective in achieving the goals of the sexual revolution. At the other end of the spectrum, the raunchy pornography of sadomasochism, bestiality and so on has a lesser cultural impact and is more widely criticized. In everyday workplace parlance the proposition is stated thusly: "I really don't mind *Playboy* so much, it's that really gross stuff that should be outlawed."

*Fortune* magazine, in the August 12, 1981 issue, commented that *Playboy* is "the only girlie magazine acceptable for family reading and display on coffee tables." This popular pornography, unlike the raunchy material, has been cleverly coupled with a world-and-life view that masquerades as a pseudo-religion attempting to restructure the human relationships necessary to civilized order.

The depictions in popular pornography cannot hastily be characterized as "filthy slime from the gutter that treats humans as animals." The photos are Madison Avenue quality; they are of beautiful women. It simply is not meaningful to equate the popular pornography with the obscure pornography. But, as we shall see, it is the popular pornography that has worked most successfully to undermine the Judeo-Christian consensus in our culture. Additionally, the obscure pornography is to a certain degree the second-generation porn, a development due to demand created by the wider acceptance of the popular pornography.

Modern pornographic man has rejected God and His law in favor of unbridled spontaneous humanism. The social restructuring caused by the pornographic philosophy has been much more subversive than the pictures themselves. Albeit, explicit pictures are an important part of the total but their crucial role is that of reassuring and comforting icons that instantaneously remind the viewer that the life-style advocated by the porn philosophy is in fact achievable. The pornographers know that the written word alone is a much slower catalyst than are explicit, easily accessible graphic reproductions of nude bodies. Simply put, a man may not reject his wife and family on the claims of written arguments. However, when you fuel the fires with erotic depictions of what awaits the liberated man, faithfulness often crumbles. There is then much more offered by the pornographers than pictures.

## THE PORNOGRAPHIC OFFER

In our era, *Playboy* is perhaps the most diabolically well-crafted lifetime manual for every possible male activity. The magazine is the ultimate higher authority for the new man. Each issue is replete with nude bodies of clean, airbrushed, almost perfect women: Women who sometimes work as nude hostesses at private pool parties; women who work for the telephone company, or who go to "Big 10" colleges; women who are willing providers of the feminine pleasures the playboy desires. The overall message is clear: Those who pose for *Playboy* are not far away, they live and work in the playboy's own neighborhood.

The magazine equips the playboy with a total life-style of clothes, expensive sports cars, stereo equipment and a cultured menu of restaurants and vacations. The *Playboy* reader is assured that he is informed, urbane, a high achiever who knows what he wants and how to get it. In the magazine's own words, "*Playboy* is a magazine of service and entertainment for men. It is designed to chronicle, interpret and shape contemporary values and life-styles."

From the beginning, *Playboy* created the general impression that its readers were a special breed of liberated males, an elite coterie of unmarried free men or at least free in spirit. The magazine was initiated to provide men with the strategic agenda for obtaining what they wanted most without paying the ultimate price of marriage.

The playboy soon learns that women are to be managed on the basis of a cost-benefit analysis. Any anxieties about or difficulties with the opposite sex can be soothed through economic power and cultural control. If the potential playboy has only limited success, each month there is a new bare-breasted, pink-skinned beauty to assure him that the playboy life-style is within reach. The initial *Playboy* offer reduced to its simplest form is, "why should men endure the slow painful death of working to support an entire family when their goals can be achieved for the price of dinner and drinks?"

The *Playboy* philosophy popularized the idea that men—to be men—no longer need to grow up, marry and support wives. The magazine dismantled the breadwinner ethic of man as provider-protector and put in its place an upwardly mobile male who selects feminine company at will from the general population. *Playboy* urged its readers to "enjoy the pleasures the female has to offer without becoming emotionally involved."

William Iverson, perhaps the most erudite *Playboy* apologist, declared:

> A mere tendency to hemophilia cannot be counted upon to ensure that men will continue to bleed for the plight of the American woman. Neither double eyelashes nor the blindness of night or

day can obscure the glaring fact that American marriage can no longer be accepted as an estate in which the sexes shall live half-slave and half-free.

*Playboy* thus appeals to man's great temptation as regards marriage: to have its benefits without its responsibilities. The effects of such thinking have after 30-plus years of *Playboy* taken their toll on the psychology of individual males, especially since readership is now around 20 million.

## FANTASY: THE DEADLY REALITY

Popular pornography must offer the reader an internal thought life that is superior to external reality. This is, of course, due to the simple fact that the playboy life-style is truly possible only for a few. The internalized images must be intense, repeated and tailored to accommodate both conscious and unconscious drives. At the same time the internal thought world must offer new experiences and variety. By accomplishing both, the pornographic culture has developed into an experiential faith that must constantly be renewed by the discovery of new opportunities.

Popular pornographic magazines, especially *Playboy* and *Penthouse* for men, and *Cosmopolitan* for women constantly offer exciting testimonies of varied new sexual experiences usually to be adopted or at least considered by the readership. *Penthouse* accomplishes this through its *Forum* section (also a separate publication). Each month numerous sexual conquests are erotically recounted to assure the reader that men and women everywhere are trying new partners, places, techniques and so on to enhance sexual experiences. In related articles, a scientific support team of medical advisors with university credentials reassures the reader that healthy sexual experience can be enhanced by wife swapping, bisexuality, cross-dressing and the like. In spite of the constant barrage of experientialism, consider the disclaimer offered by *Playboy*:

> The contemporary psychiatrist knows, and will gladly tell any who care to listen that books and pictures and pamphlets and papers that deal openly and honestly with sex have little or no effect upon human behavior and whatever effect they do have is healthful, rather than injurious.

*Cosmopolitan*, although tamer, provides the same experiential enthusiasm for women. Articles such as "Can Adultery Save Your Marriage?" and "Is He the Right Lover?" appear in every issue.

The social costs of experiential faith have been tremendous, especially in the area of divorce. Once the playboy commits himself to new experiences, the cost-benefit analysis of monogamous sexuality begins to slowly undermine marriage. The playboy asks himself "why put up with all that marriage requires when new sexual encounters are so easily attained?" The magazines promise that until the man actually breaks away, pornography will see him through. The economic aspect to all this cannot be minimized. Polls taken among judges who deal with domestic relations indicate that the major cause in divorce is radical disagreement about family finances. Playboy offers the reader a different way to think about how to spend money. It simply is cheaper to obtain sex than to enhance the growth and development of a family.

The economics of sexuality in the *Playboy* world must be understood in the context of the type of sex that popular pornography has in mind. The goal in pornographic sex is not a multidimensional empathetic relationship but mere achievement of orgasm. A marriage relationship is expensive both economically and personally. The playboy is told that only orgasm is important and orgasm is far less costly than marriage.

One genre of pornographic literature helps support the experiential faith by providing classified ads in which individuals can attract the like-minded. The Senate Judiciary Committee has in its files examples of such publications that include child advertisers who sell their services to adults. The usual case, however, is simply wife swapping, threesomes and other so-called recreational variations.

There is a psychological cost to the experiential faith of pornography. The participant must find new and more intense stimuli. New horizons must be tested. A couple of years ago, San Francisco newspapers reported that one in ten homicides in that city were related to homosexual sado-masochistic practices. In seeking the ultimate experience, homosexuals were flirting with death itself as they participated in a bizarre mixture of sexual stimulation and pain. Once the pornographic offer of experiential faith is accepted, it becomes increasingly difficult to find a new experience, short of flirting with death.

## THE SMOTHERING OF REAL IDENTITY

There is also a de-individualizing result that flows from repeated exposure to pornography. Month after month of exposure to erotic nudity tends to blur the entirety of all women into an undifferentiated whole. The pornographic man, because of so much intense emotional exposure to pornography, simply finds himself unable to concentrate on one woman. Psychologists have found that the popular pornography has tended to produce this result more than obscure porn. This is because the Playmate-of-the-Month has such an intense fantasy impact on the reader. She serves as a reminder that ultimate and perfect sex is everywhere for the playboy. The raunchy porn, while arousing, does not seem to create the same longing or desire.

The same lack of concentration on one woman that grows out of extended stimuli from pornographic materials also occurs in the form of sexual disinterest. Studies have shown that X-rated adult theaters are the most harmful here. In a relatively short time frame, the viewer is exposed to numerous erotic encounters, often involving a small group of characters. What may take several days to film is all packed together in 90 minutes. The viewer receives the message loud and clear: what is happening on the screen cannot happen in marriage. A sexual relationship with only one partner who is limited by space and time and human energy simply cannot live up to the fantasy of the adult film.

## FICTIONALIZING YOUR LIFE

This psychological harm caused by pornography has been termed the "will of fiction." Pornography is the perfect material for the man who desires to live his life in a world of imagination; he accepts the role of the voyeur. Man's inner private world becomes the secret place to live out all the opportunities offered in pornography. In this private world, man is omnipotent; he can fantasize about any and all sexual partners. In Rushdoony's words, "The pornographic imagination prefers the inner world of the imagination, where the ability to manipulate people without challenge or failure and without consequence reigns undisturbed by reality."

The experiential faith promoted by the popular pornographers has both trickled up and trickled down. Most popular movies and television shows enthusiastically support the idea that man must embrace a faithful search for new experiences. On the other hand, the increased demand for obscure pornography is of course the logical next step down in the quest for an untested experience.

## SEX WITHOUT PERSONS

Perhaps the most tragic harm caused by pornography is its destruction of sex itself. Pornography, upon developing an experiential faith and a "will to fiction," multiplies real or imagined sex partners to such an extent that mutuality in a monogamous relationship becomes boring, uneventful and very difficult. Sex becomes possible with a variety of persons. Promiscuity becomes the goal. If a partner cannot be found? Then pornography is substituted as a stimulus and masturbation as an outlet. Since orgasm and new experience is the goal in the porn culture, the partner becomes less and less important. Greg Bahnsen has termed this development "sex without persons." Bahnsen points out that true sexuality cannot survive the sexual (or pornographic) revolution, because true sexuality requires mutuality of care and tenderness in a marital relationship. The "sex without persons" culture can and does have lots of orgasms, but true sexuality within marriage must be rejected.

The articles in *Playboy* during the 1960s helped promote the idea that sex must be given freely in a spontaneous existential moment, not within the context of a long-term commitment with one particular person. Rod McKuen's "Gentle on My Mind" is a song in praise of a noncommittal relationship between a man and a woman in which the singer expresses his pleasure in not being shackled to his partner by a marriage license. Sex then, to be good, must be found outside the formal legal commitment of marriage.

A graphic example of "sex without persons" is the peep show adult bookstore where pornographic films are shown in private booths for 25¢ per 2-minute segment. The pornographic man views these films as masturbation stimulation. In Los Angeles, the City Council ordered the self-locking doors removed from the viewing booths because random homosexual acts were so commonplace inside the bookstores. As pornography promotes "sex without persons," orgasm is elevated to the ultimate beatitude. Men who cannot achieve the fantasy dream of the *Playboy* mansion settle instead for oral homosexual sex in a peep show booth.

## THE TARGETING OF CHILDREN

"Sex without persons" has logically developed into sex with the easiest person to exploit. This means that the most dependent persons in our society, children, are now in season. The Rene Guyon Society is a pro-incest, pro-child sex organization whose motto is "sex before eight or its too late." The North American Man-Boy Love Association (NAMBLA) publication features child pornography and explicit stories about adult encounters with young boys. These groups and others like them represent a growing counter-culture movement of child sex-exploitation.

The popular pornographers also promote child porn and exploitation. *Penthouse* has featured pictorials in which adults are made to look like children. Both *Playboy* and *Penthouse* used full-page cartoons to promote child abuse. One *Playboy* cartoon featured a little girl walking out of a room turning to a stereotypical "dirty old man" and exclaiming, "You call that molesting?" Sex between children and Santa Claus is a seasonal favorite. It is no wonder that Hugh Hefner's favorite song is "Thank Heaven for Little Girls." Preoccupation with and legitimization of sex with children has subtly appeared in popular women's magazines such as *Harper's Bazaar* and *Cosmopolitan* with prepubescent children featured in provocative poses, advertising such items as perfume.

Seth Goldstein, an inspector with the District Attorney in Santa Clara, California, writes:

> Most pedophiles operate within their own neighborhoods; they don't go out seeking the services of child prostitutes. Some subscribe to the underground publications and correspondence which supply them with a ready number of child victims. One article appearing in an underground sex publication explained how a child molester could acquire access to children by volunteering to become involved in programs dealing with children, noting that access is not only easy to obtain but such participation by adults is encouraged. In 1977, an official of Boy Scouts of America (BSA) was charged with various pornography and delinquency violations. He had been recruiting children from his job at a local YMCA. Found in his apartment were 5,000 pictures and slides of children as young as 2 years old. Investigators reported that he had worked for the BSA for 5 years.

In San José, California, a large child pornography ring was exposed which had an international mailing list. The network was exchanging photographs, video cassettes, films and even children themselves. A study conducted by the Illinois Legislative Investigatory Commission revealed that most child pornography is sold through mail order.

## AGGRESSION AGAINST WOMEN

Sexual aggression against women is increasingly linked with pornography. Many researchers now believe that as the fantasy world of pornographic imagination opens up one taboo, that of forbidden sex, and if the added dimension of sadomasochistic scenes are added, there is similar breakdown of the inhibitions against rape. FBI expert Ken Lanning reports that in cases of rape or rape and murder, the investigation frequently reveals that the perpetrator owns a large and elaborate library of pornography. A computer study done by the Michigan State Police found that in 40 percent of all sexual assault cases, pornography was involved just prior to the act or during the act. The obscene phone call is often a middle ground on the path from porn fantasy to sexual aggression. Studies have shown that the caller frequently has a pornographic magazine open as the call is made.

One pornographic business, High Society, owned by Gloria Leonard, operates an obscene phone call service consisting of various 30-second prerecorded messages. The caller hears a sensuous female voice requesting sexually aggressive acts. The voice pretends to act out a sexual encounter and responds as though she enjoys abuse. Each call leads to another more graphic message, and there is evidence that local telephone companies are splitting the profits from this call service with the pornographic businesses.

## CRIME AND PORN: THE HELLISH MARRIAGE

The mixing of erotica and violence has become increasingly the subject of scientific study. For example, Dr. Neil Malamuts of the University of Manitoba has been testing his subjects by exposing them to violent pornography. The level of aggression in males was substantially increased by such exposure. These studies reveal that the so-called victimless crime of pornography has as its victims women and children. Linda Lovelace, who played the lead in the film *Deep Throat*, talks of being beaten and drugged into submission and forced to act out her part. She recalls that the film's producers did not even bother to use make-up to cover the bruises on her legs.

In a study presented to the American Society of Criminology, University of New Hampshire, researchers claimed that a direct correlation exists between a state's per capita rapes and percentage of male-magazine readers.

## THE ATTACK ON COMMUNITIES

Pornograhy harms individuals in the larger context of their neighborhoods and communities. It is estimated that the gross sales of the porn industry are $6 billion. There are approximately 18,000 adult bookstores in the United States. The Adult Film Association of America boasts 800 affiliated movie houses. In 1981 there were 6 million video cassettes sold in the United States, 20 percent were porn. On cable television there are 12 late night porn film services. There are approximately 80 *Penthouse, Playboy, Hustler* type magazines that are sold in convenience food stores and on newsstands. In short, pornography is part of the warp and woof of our neighborhood business environment. The profit pressure for porn is enormous. Law enforcement officials estimate that organized crime controls half of the pornography industry. Only gambling and narcotics bring in more revenue.

Organized crime uses local adult establishments to launder money from other illegal operations. Other related organized crimes seem to proliferate in areas where several adult outlets exist. Prostitution and narcotics pushing soon take hold. Municipalities frequently commission studies of land use and zoning of adult business to decide how best to regulate the concentration level. In New York, which followed a plan that called for high concentration of porn business in one neighborhood, a 70 percent increase in rape, robbery and assault occurred. A Phoenix study concluded that property values, financial policies of banks, and crime were affected by the city's concentration of adult bookstores.

## THE POLITICS OF THE PORNOGRAPHY INDUSTRY

The pornography industry also has a little-known impact on the general welfare of our national political decisions. Playboy Foundation provided the initial grant to Keith Stroup to create the National Organization for Reform of Marijuana Laws.

In 1979 *Playboy* founded an in-depth legal and "scientific" analysis of cocaine, with glowing encouragements. The study has been used successfully in court to challenge convictions, using a strategy based on the theory that cocaine is not a narcotic.

- *Playboy* has provided significant funding for the Center for Constitutional Rights, headed by former Attorney Ramsey Clark and which has repeatedly served as a legal defense team for international terrorists.
- P.E.N. International Club also supports terrorist activity and is a recipient of funds from pornographic publishers and businesses.
- *Penthouse* funds the radical Viet Nam Veterans of America, a group that actively supported Ho Chi Minh and now maintains formal ties with Hanoi. Many members of *Playboy* and *Hustler* organizations are former members of or have ties to the Yippie movement of the late 60s and early 70s.

*Playboy* also has been a long time supporter of the feminist movement and until recently, women's groups welcomed the contributions with open arms. Hugh Hefner loaned his *Playboy* mansion in Los Angeles for a fundraiser for the National Organization for Women, raising $25,000.

The Playboy Foundation donor list looks like an honor

role of the social Left. Nearly all major gay rights organizations receive a grant of some kind. The ACLU, receiving $50,000 in 1982, heads the list of Playboy grantees. Playboy also makes its talented art department available for activist causes. People for the American Way and the National Council to Control Handguns both have received free advertising and art work.

Playboy Foundation has used its grants and liberal editorial policy to create an intellectual, left-leaning coalition that generally supports the magazine. Consider the language of a grant request letter written by Laura Lederer to *Playboy* on behalf of Women Against Violence in Pornography and Media: "Playboy magazine has always been in the front lines of the country's social problems . . . *Playboy* has always been interested in healthy, happy relations between the sexes." Ironic isn't it? An anti-porn group embracing *Playboy* while asking for a grant to fight porn. Their similar political plans for the United States makes such odd alliances more understandable.

The connection of pornography and organized crime goes together with lobbying efforts to legalize marijuana and cocaine. Playboy Forum is the self-proclaimed drug lobby in the United States. During 1966 and 1967, Hugh Hefner conducted an on-going dialogue with Timothy Leary, whose great contribution was an article entitled, "LSD and Sex." It is not surprising that radical intellectuals with ties to revolutionary organizations have shown up at *Playboy* in a steady flow.

The popular porn industry has developed into a comprehensive cultural agenda. Social activists look to *Playboy* for leadership and money. Frustrated males read stories and look at pictures and fantasize about freedom from commitment to marriage or take action and simply divorce their wives who they decide are too much trouble. Like all revolutionary movements, popular porn is not enough for some. Child molesting and rape soon become the easier alternative to the *Playboy* life-style just as it, in turn, was easier than marriage. We have entered the "sex without persons" mentality that has enabled June Singer to comment about masturbation:

> There is greater freedom in knowing that one can be whole in one's inner life and that this wholeness need not depend absolutely upon a relationship with another person.

Orgasm has become the goal of the popular pornographers. Yet "orgasm" is used as a *political* battlecry. It should always be remembered that what *Playboy, Penthouse* and *Cosmopolitan* intend to do is equip the pornographic man and woman with a total culture to assist him in achieving the quality of life desired. The magazines are replete with counseling, liberal politics, consumer items and guides to creative hedonistic living.

The merging of all these elements makes it an error to call the popular porn "dirty pictures." *Playboy* is actually a very seductive and attractive life-style that has gained widespread acceptance. For this reason it is the popular pornography that represents the greatest threat to our civilization. Pornography is far more than dirty pictures. It is the foundation for a world view that educates, titilates and stimulates men and women into tragically deadly illusion.

### RESPONSIBLE CITIZEN INVOLVEMENT

As an aware and concerned individual, you can do a great deal to help stem the tide of the pornographic revolution. The following suggestions are constructive, positive approaches you can utilize in helping to eliminate the impact of popular pornography.

1. Take responsibility for your own neighborhood and city by forming a group in your church or civic organization to work and study together.

2. If you purchase a major item such as an automobile or stereo, send a copy of the receipt to the manufacturer and explain that you disapprove of advertising in *Playboy, Penthouse, Cosmopolitan,* etc. The post-purchase technique is the most effective for major purchases.

3. Ask your group to save purchase receipts from your local grocery or drugstore for two months. Arrange a meeting with the manager and politely present the receipts to him and request that the offensive material be removed. Explain that young cashiers should not be required to sell such magazines over the counter.

4. Find out if local pornography establishments (bookstores, massage parlors, etc.) accept major credit cards. Arrange a meeting between representatives of your group and the bank that handles the credit card account. Remind the bank official of the numbers of your group that have accounts with the bank. Ask that the bank cancel the credit cards that support pornography.

5. Contact your city councilman and request that he sponsor a zoning/land use study on the effects of adult business on the crime rate, real estate values and local businesses. Meet with real estate developers who operate in the area surrounding adult business and enlist their support.

6. Insist that the local prosecutor prosecute adult businesses as a public nuisance. Atlanta, Georgia has removed 40 adult businesses under this strategy.

7. Find a local zip code chairman as a contact person so that letter writing can be targeted to stores in a neighborhood. Letters from across town are not as effective.

8. Ask your doctor not to place prescriptions in drug stores that are uncooperative about removing magazines.

9. Attend trials when child molesters, rapists or adult businesses are involved. Your presence will let the judge know that you care about your community and about his approach to pornography. Incidentally, his judgeship could be an election issue next time around. You may want to keep track of his record and even publicize in newsletters how your judges rule.

10. Invite local lawyers or public officials to speak at a dinner on the general subject of pornography. Create a mutually beneficial relationship by making an annual award to the local official who has done the most to help your efforts.

11. Lobby the city council and mayor's offices not to accept cable programming contracts that include pornographic movies.

12. Publicize a list of local stores that refuse to sell pornography. Have members of your group reinforce the manager's decision by communicating why you chose that particular store. Develop a similar list of businesses that have withdrawn from *Playboy*.

13. Contact one of the following groups for assistance:
   • Chicago Statement Foundation
      P.O. Box 40945
      Washington, D.C. 20016
      This group is a major source of information on *Playboy*. The group was successful in convincing Florsheim Shoes to withdraw advertisements from *Playboy*.
   • National Federation for Decency
      Drawer 2440
      Tupeleo, MS 38803
      This group is the best source for information on advertisers and for update media reviews. Journal subscription of $15.00 per year is well worth the investment.

- Citizens for Decency through Law
  2331 W. Royal Palm Road, #105
  Phoenix, AZ 85021

This group is well known for its legal work in obscenity cases.

---

## Study Questions

1. What is the biblical view of man's imagination? How is man responsible to God for his thoughts? How does the Bible explain the eventual externalizing of the internal thought life?

2. Study and explain why God forbade the Israelites from intermarrying with idolatrous cultures. How does sexuality seduce people into a new cultural outlook?

3. Examine the Song of Songs and other appropriate passages to develop a biblical view of sex.

4. Why does God use powerful sexual imagery to describe spiritual idolatry? Is pornography the merger of sexual and spiritual idolatry?

5. What does "given over to a reprobate mind" mean in Romans 1?

---

## About the Author

March Bell is a graduate of the Pepperdine University School of Law. He was formerly Counsel to the Senate Subcommittee on Security and Terrorism. While with the subcommittee, he developed the forfeiture and reporting provisions of H.R. 3635, The Child Protection Act of 1984. That bill, signed into law by President Reagan, allows prosecutions of child pornography without having to prove that the material is "obscene." The forfeiture provisions allow courts to seize the profits and assets of a child porn operation.

Mr. Bell is now Executive Director of the Rutherford Institute, a foundation that participates in First Amendment and civil rights law.

# 7

# RELIGIOUS FREEDOM AND THE PUBLIC SCHOOLS

by
Samuel E. Ericsson

No area of concern today causes greater confusion for Christians than that which relates to religious activities in the public schools. A major reason for the confusion is that many United States Supreme Court decisions on the subject have been miscommunicated, misinterpreted and misapplied. The common thread running through the various Supreme Court decisions on religious activities in public schools is this: state-initiated, school-sponsored and teacher-led religious instruction or religious exercises violate the Establishment Clause of the First Amendment. In brief, the public school teacher should not serve as a priest or minister in the classroom. However, the Supreme Court has never declared that students may not voluntarily initiate and conduct meetings with religious content during their free time on the school campus.

A review of the most significant church-state cases over the past 40 years indicates that the United States Supreme Court has sought, in large part, to preserve the institutional separation of church and state while recognizing that there are some overlapping areas of competing claims and interests. We will briefly review some of the major decisions in this area:

1. Public schools cannot force students to participate in activities that violate their religious convictions. Parents can effectively object on behalf of their children to any participation in activities that are contrary to their religious convictions. This is particularly important on issues touching controversial subjects such as sex education. What biblical principles apply in this case?

2. The public schools cannot teach "The Faith." In 1948, in Illinois, many public schools provided religious indoctrination as part of their regular curriculum. Religious instructors went directly to the classroom, dismissed any nonparticipating students and proceeded to teach The Faith. These instructors were under the direct supervision of school administrators, who also controlled the religious content of the classes.

The Supreme Court held that the state, through its public schools and teachers, should not teach a specific faith, whether it be Catholicism, Protestantism, Judaism, Mormonism or any other "ism." It concluded that this responsibility resides primarily with the family and the Church. In effect, the Court said that "equipping the saints" and "nurturing the saints" is not the official business of the state. What does the Bible say on this point?

3. The state should accommodate the spiritual needs of school children. Although the state may not directly get involved in teaching a given faith, the Supreme Court upheld a program in New York whereby public schoolchildren were released for religious instruction during the school day. The instruction took place away from the school campus and was taught by religious instructors supervised by churches and parents, wholly independent from state supervision.

In that case, the Supreme Court noted that Americans

are a religious people and that our public institutions presuppose the existence of a Supreme Being. The public schools should accommodate the spiritual needs of schoolchildren by working with churches, synagogues and parents to provide, during the school day, an opportunity for religious instruction.

Although "released time religious education" has been available to Christians for most of this century, very few Protestants, particularly evangelicals, take advantage of this great opportunity. In New York City in 1984, out of the more than 30,000 children released each Wednesday afternoon between 2:00 and 3:00 for released time religious education, only five percent are Protestant. The opportunity is there. The challenge is to put it to use.

4. Official state-composed prayers for students are out. In 1962, the Supreme Court declared unconstitutional a 22-word prayer written by the Regents of the State of New York for their public school children. In this oft-criticized case, the Supreme Court simply said that it is not the appropriate business of the state to compose prayers for anyone, including children. There continues to be an effort by some Christians to reverse this decision.

5. Public school teachers should not lead in devotional exercises. The issue of religion in public schools boiled over in 1963 in the famous case involving Madelyn Murray O'Hair and her son, William. She and others challenged laws in Maryland and Pennsylvania which allowed public school teachers to lead children in devotional exercises at the beginning of the school day. The issue facing the Court in this case was whether it is an appropriate function of the state to direct its public school teachers to conduct religious exercises. The Supreme Court concluded that public school teachers should not serve as ministers or priests in the classroom leading in such exercises.

This decision caused much debate and confusion. The

central question, of course, is to what extent the state should formally become involved in religious matters. The Supreme Court has indicated that it is appropriate for the state to acknowledge the existence and sovereignty of God. Thus, our motto, "In God We Trust" is appropriately inscribed on our coins and our pledge of allegiance states, "One Nation, Under God." Contrary to widespread belief, the motto "In God We Trust" did not become the official U.S. motto until 1956, and the phrase "One Nation, Under God" was added officially by Congress to the pledge in 1953.

Although it may be appropriate to acknowledge God's existence and sovereignty in an official way, is this the same as worshiping Him? Many Christians are troubled by having non-believers lead their children in worshiping a God in whom they do not believe. Is it biblical for a nonbelieving teacher to lead children in a worship of God? Is this true worship, civil religion or mere hypocrisy? To many, this is seen as the central issue in the "school prayer debate."

Although the Supreme Court declared that teachers should not lead morning devotions, the Supreme Court made it quite clear in the same decision that the objective study of the Bible, such as in literature or history or of comparative religion as part of a secular program of education did not violate the First Amendment. In order to pass constitutional standards, such programs need to be carefully developed to protect against proselytizing in the classroom.

No doubt, most Christians would object to a teacher, a member of a cult, using the classroom as a platform to proselytize students to his or her religion. We should be equally sensitive to those non-Christian parents who object to Christians seeking to take advantage of their position in the classroom. A helpful "rule" on many of these issues was laid down by Christ when He taught: "Whatever you want others to do for you, do so for them; for this is the Law and the Prophets" (Matt. 7:12, *NASB*).

James Panoch and David Barr, advocates of religious education in the public schools, contend, "The school teaches religion whether it teaches religion or not . . . . One way or the other it teaches something about religion." The authors insist the school that excludes religion teaches by inference that religion is not an important area of concern for students. To exclude religion from study on the grounds of "neutrality" is, as they suggest, to "confuse neutrality with sterility." The Supreme Court has not removed religion from the public schools, Panoch and Barr insist: "We did. Uninformed teachers, an unconcerned public, unconscious churchmen—all have their hand in systematically eliminating all mention of the Bible and religion from significant areas of school life." Christians should carefully re-evaluate the opportunities available in the public schools.

6. Public schools may give equal access to secondary school students. As noted above, the landmark Supreme Court decisions in the early 1960s invalidated state-composed prayers and state initiated, school sponsored and teacher-led religious exercises. The touchstone in both cases was the official support given to religious exercises by the state and local school authorities and teachers.

The Supreme Court did not, however, intend to prohibit truly voluntary, student-initiated and student-run religious activities on public school property. Indeed, the Supreme Court has stated that the public schools should accommodate the religious needs of students. One way to accommodate those spiritual needs is to allow for released time religious education. This is ideal for elementary schools. However, at the secondary school level a more effective means of accommodating the spiritual needs of students during the school day is to allow them to meet on their own time for meetings with religious content.

Tragically, as part of the fallout from the reaction to the decisions in the early 1960s, some local school boards, administrators and eventually some lower courts began to believe the rhetoric flowing from many corners that the Supreme Court had forbidden *all* "voluntary prayer" in public schools. The waters became thoroughly muddied when the often-heard response to this false statement was that children could pray individually and silently, such as before a math exam, so long as no one seemed bothered by the bowing of the head.

Both of these extremes were mistaken and both overlooked the critical difference between teacher-led "voluntary" religious exercise and student-initiated and student-run meetings with religious content. Gradually, school district after school district began to adopt policies that closed the door to religious expression among students in all but the most perfunctory settings.

The momentum for denying equal access for religious expression accelerated significantly after a 1980 decision by a lower court which declared that a wholly voluntary student-initiated and student-run meeting with religious content among eight students before school and behind closed doors was "too dangerous to permit"! Why? The Court felt that some naive student might somehow mistakenly conclude that these eight students were establishing some form of religion which had the "official" blessing of the school. The school did not identify any students that were that naive and gullible.

The decision barring the eight students from meeting conflicts with a decision by the Supreme Court involving students in public universities. In a 1981 case, *Widmar* v. *Vincent,* a group of college students at the University of

Missouri wanted equal access to the use of university facilities for a time of prayer, Bible study and worship. Over 100 other nonreligious student groups were meeting in other available facilities. The Christians simply wanted equal access. When the public university denied such access, the students went to court and won. The Supreme Court declared that a public university may not deny voluntary groups equal access to the use of university facilities based upon the religious content of their speech. Moreover, the Supreme Court declared that worship is a form of protected speech.

The decision by the Supreme Court affirming equal access in public universities was extended in 1983 by a lower federal court to students at the high school level. Although there remains some conflict in the lower courts on this particular issue, most constitutional scholars believe that high school students cannot be discriminated against on the basis of the religious content of their speech in voluntary student-initiated and student-run meetings. These meetings can truly meet the spiritual needs of many students on campus during the school day. Often the real need of students in the schools is not simply for the academic content of a well-structured Bible study but for the spiritual support of other Christian students who often find themselves in an environment saturated with non-Christian attitudes, philosophies and activities. Equal access provides an opportunity for such spiritual support groups.

Finally, we must not overlook the impact that Christian teachers have as they live their witness on public school campuses. If only ten percent of public school teachers are born-again believers, then there are over 200,000 Christian teachers in our nation. Rather than being affirmed and encouraged by other Christians for their commitment to public service, they are often on the receiving end of the onslaught of criticism heaped on public schools. It was in large part, because of teachers like Mr. Sandberg in my elementary school, Mr. Roulette in junior high and Mrs. Maxfield in high school that I, for one, saw that Christianity was "real."

There are currently 36 million children in the public schools, a number greater than the aggregate population of the 24 African nations. Tragically, many Christians today express less concern for these millions of children and their Christian teachers than is shown for foreign missions.

The issue of religion in the public school may be summed up in the following "pair words," developed by James V. Panoch:

- The school may sponsor the *study* of religion, but may not sponsor the *practice* of religion.
- The school may *expose* students to all religious views, but may not *impose* any particular view.
- The school's approach to religion is one of *instruction,* not one of *indoctrination.*
- The function of the school is to *educate* about all, not to *convert* to any one religion.
- The school's approach to religion is *academic* not *devotional.*
- The school should *study* what all people believe, but should not *teach* a pupil what he should believe.
- The school should strive for student *awareness* of all religions, but should not press for student *acceptance* of any one religion.
- The school should seek to *inform* the student about various beliefs, but should not seek to *conform* him to any one belief.

As Christians, we need to be both constructive and

discerning as well as faithful in exercising our constitutional freedoms and utilizing the opportunities available to us in the public schools. Then our children, our schools and, consequently, our nation will be the better for our having done so.

---

## Study Questions

1. To what extent should public school teachers be allowed to share their faith in the classroom?

2. At what point does the government have a compelling interest to become involved in curriculum, policies or practices of church-operated Christian schools?

3. To what extent should the government acknowledge a particular religion as "official"?

4. To what extent is it appropriate to "legislate morality"?

5. Is it possible to teach the Bible "objectively" to the public schools if the teacher is a Christian? A non-Christian?

## Suggested Readings

Buzzard, Lynn R. and Ericsson, Samuel E. *The Battle for Religious Liberty.* Elgin, IL: David C. Cook Publishing Company, 1982.

Buzzard, Lynn R. Schools: *They Haven't Got a Prayer.* Elgin, IL: David C. Cook Publishing Company, 1982.

Buzzard, Lynn R. and Eck, Laury. *Tell It to the Church.* Elgin, IL: David C. Cook Publishing Company, 1982.

Buzzard, Lynn R. and Ericsson, Samuel E. *With Liberty and Justice*. Wheaton, IL: Victor Books, 1984.

Neuhaus, Richard John. *Christian Faith and Public Policy*. Minneapolis, MN: Augsburg Publishing House, 1977.

Piediscalzi, Nicholas and Collie, William E. *Teaching About Religion in Public Schools*. Allen, TX: Argus, 1977.

## About the Author
Samuel E. Ericsson is the director for the Center for Law and Religious Freedom of the Christian Legal Society and directs the CLS Washington, D.C. office. The Center serves as a resource on church-state issues for members of the branches of government and the religious community. Sam is a graduate of the University of Southern California and Harvard Law School. He practiced law for ten years with a major Los Angeles law firm and served for four years as coordinator of ministries at Grace Community Church in Sun Valley, California. He is the co-author of *The Battle for Religious Liberty* (David C. Cook) and *With Liberty and Justice* (Victor Books). A member of the California State Bar and the American Bar Association, he resides in Springfield, Virginia with his wife Bobby and their two children.

# 8

# THE HALL OF DEADLY MIRRORS
## Peace and Nuclear Arms
by
Charles W. Jarvis

The amusement park hawker draws you like a magnet to the ticket counter. You nervously pay, despite his somber warning crackling through a bad P.A. system, "Some never come out of the hall of mirrors." Once inside, you bump your way through the maze. Moments of panic mix with the thrill of fear. At the exit, looking quickly back, you tell yourself, "That wasn't so bad!"

Evangelicals are now caught in a hall of deadly mirrors; strategy, peace and nuclear arms seem to crisscross, and the temptation to step into deadly illusion is immense. Is there no exit, no way back? We fantasize that the next strategic turn will be less threatening, less befuddling. Detente will solve our problems; arms control can stop the madness; a new defense technology will finally checkmate the opposition.

As stewards of the Word of Life, evangelicals have often shown great determination and exactness when dealing with matters of faith and doctrine, but take us out of the sanctuary into the political arena and we hem and haw, finally spouting whatever political fashion is near at hand or on the rise. When analyzing peace and nuclear arms issues, evangelicals have the sacred duty to apply themselves with the same dedication that we give to such personal and spiritual concerns as the family, morality or evangelism. The stakes are high and the implications are extraordinary. We need, therefore, to discern the varieties of "peace" now offered us.

## PEACE vs. PEACE vs. PEACE
### The Scriptural Structure of Peace

In Hebrew, the word *shalom* means "peace" and has a variety of rich meanings. The root word means "solidity," "wholeness," "well-being" and can suggest "prosperity," "integrity" and "physical health" as well. The many implications of shalom lead us to look beyond the intimation of decay in our world to the promised restoration of all things.

Can a degree of shalom be evident in our secular age and "humanistic" culture? Not only *can* it be revealed, it *must* be! The Christian tradition has established, not only a priestly role for the church, but also prophetic and kingly responsibilities, providing political and social institutions with a "word fitly spoken."

The thread of cultural responsibility is clearly discernable from Genesis through this age, and the mandate is stark and convincing—God's Word is to be applied in our time, in our lives, in our nation and in every realm of the world. Since we are stewards of the harmony and peace of our society (Rom. 14:17-18; 1 Cor. 7:15) we should encourage and refine our political systems. Our calling presumes that our standards are derived from the Scriptures. And much of the debate over defense, arms and peace might be resolved if we would admit to our sometimes dangerously editorial interpretations of the Scriptures. "Peace" is no exception.

## The Soviet Concept of "Peace"

The Russian word *mir* is commonly translated as "peace." Mir, however, is a complex term. It refers first to the world: the planet and all its inhabitants. Only in a secondary sense does it refer to concord among people and nations or the absence of hostility.[1]

When the Bolshevik Revolution began to solidify its power *mir* took on an ideological meaning. Now it refers primarily to the conditions of Marxist-Leninist society, which are all considered "just and good and right." Only the Soviet Union and other Marxist states can enjoy *mir*. The source of all wars and hostility is "democratic capitalist imperialism," which is the sole obstacle to the fulfillment of the holy mission of the peaceful socialist world system: establishing mir in all other societies of the world. Picture the peoples of the world under the heavy yoke of democracy and authoritarianism, yearning for Marxist liberation and genuine, total mir. Peace, in the Soviet view, is part and parcel to the Marxist-Leninist world order.

In 1917, Lenin stated categorically that only revolutionary states can enjoy mir, and there is no mir possible between Marxist and non-Marxist states. The only possibility is a strategic cessation of hostilities.

Sanakoyev declares, "There can be no political or moral basis for an antiwar movement that is directed against the policy of the socialist governments, because (the latter) consistently pursue the policy of peace (mir), meeting the vital interests of the peoples and therefore enjoying their unreserved approval."[2]

Warfare is necessarily linked in the Marxist mind to peace. Georgi Dimitrov reinforces the combative nature of mir-peace: "To want peace (mir) is not enough. It is necessary to fight for peace. The struggle for peace is a struggle against capitalism, a struggle for the victory of socialism throughout the world."[3] In other words, the

Soviets see themselves "waging peace," ever "struggling to realize worldwide Marxism." Peace to them means domination of all ideas by one ideal—world mir.

The vision is total and the implications for military action are unlimited. "No weapon as such, including the nuclear weapon, determines the social character of the war . . . the war on the part of the socialist states will be a just war regardless of the type of weapons employed."[4]

Evidence is very strong that Soviet military strategists believe nuclear war can be fought and won under "proper condition" of Soviet strength. The overarching vision of Marxian Peace-Utopia (mir) still fires the minds as well as the ICBMs and bombers of Soviet strategists. Mir is thought to be an historically determined fact to be realized.

Marches in the West are translated as mass pleas for the Marxist victory. Lenin ridiculed what he called "the social ministers and opportunists who are always ready to build dreams of future peaceful socialism." Pragmatically dedicated as they are, the Soviets believe that "with all the inconsistency of the pacifists, their campaign against nuclear war . . . is of enormous significance in defining the tactics of communist parties in the struggle for peace (mir) and socialism . . . . "[5]

## Secular Visions of Peace

Lacking the foundation of ethics, the two humanist extremes in the West—the pragmatic pacifists and the pragmatic defenders—snipe verbally at each other, but hope for strangely similar ends: personal peace and material well-being for all (or most). Absolute good and absolute evil are only distant memories from faded college texts or childhood catechisms. Values are in disarray.

The pragmatic pacifists, taking their cue from Marxist socio-economists, categorically blame the West, particularly the U.S., for nearly every problem. The pragmatic defenders, forgetting that only a transcendent ethic will sustain communities for very long, glorify the decadence of the West as a necessity and, therefore, a positive good worthy of any and all sacrifice.

Pragmatic pacifists are convinced the Soviet Leninists are "really just like us." Pragmatic defenders disdain Socialist power structures, not because of some inherent moral repugnance toward "planning," but because such structures "repress free expression, such as leisure life, sexual orientation or aesthetic pleasure."

No greater horror should transfix us than the possibility that one or the other of the secular utopias should come to pass. Certainly there is more to life than this confusing soap opera that entrances the West. If defense of the nation is valid, that defense must grow out of a clear and convincing plan for bringing societal reformation and revitalization.

## NUCLEAR DEFENSE AND EVANGELICAL OPINION

Evangelicals seriously involved in the nuclear arms debate present two overarching views of nuclear defense, Moral Deterrent Defense and Moral Disarmament. Each of those positions includes groups with differing opinions about certain aspects of defense. We will examine each, identifying some of their theological, strategic and historical assumptions.

### Moral Deterrent Defense

1. *Theological Assumptions:* Evangelicals are often first attracted to the Moral Deterrent position because of their theological repudiation of Mutual Assured Destruction (MAD). That nuclear strategy, first articulated by Defense Secretary Robert McNamara under President

Kennedy, has been the prevailing defense strategy of the United States until the Reagan Administration. Briefly, MAD strategists envisioned the creation of a nuclear stalemate by targeting civilian populations in the Soviet Union. They actively negotiated with and encouraged (by restraining U.S. strategic development) the Soviets to reciprocate. Effectively, population centers have been held as nuclear hostages. The ethical implications of that strategy are clear from even a cursory glance at the historic criteria for a just war: (1) a just cause; (2) no alternative to violence; (3) properly constituted authority; (4) a feasible goal; (5) action proportionate to the threat; and (6) reconciliation is sought. Moral Deterrent Defenders call MAD into question while seeking other alternatives to unilateral disarmament.

The Moral Deterrent Defense is founded on the classical biblical view of the state, which presumes government to be a "servant of God" and a "minister of God." Those "religious" titles, found in Romans 13, should alert us to the fact that governments are to act according to the ethical standards by which they will one day be judged. The civil authority "does not bear the sword for nothing" (Rom. 13:4, *NASB*) and thus, the morality of some forms of threatening action is supported under the classical interpretation. If civil threat and punishment are presumed to be allowed domestically, Moral Deterrent supporters suggest that defense of our political community is supportable, if appropriately framed by ethical standards. Nuclear weapons aimed primarily at population centers are ethically repugnant, so thus the Moral Deterrent school seeks other options that effectively deter or inhibit Soviet military action.

2. *Strategic Assumptions:* The Moral Deterrent school views itself as attempting to apply moral principles in a world of hard realities. The litany of strategic facts pre-

sented by this school sobers any analyst:

• The United States froze deployment of its B-52 bomber force in 1962 and those numbers have dwindled since then; the Soviets have deployed more than 230 intercontinental-range Backfire bombers and will soon deploy the Blackjack bomber.

• The United States froze deployment of new strategic submarines (SSBN) from 1969 to 1982; the Soviets deployed six new classes of SSBNs involving 62 new strategic submarines during the same period.

• The United States deployed only one new strategic submarine missile (SLBM) during the last 13 years; the Soviets deployed five new types, involving hundreds of new missiles during the same period.

• The United States deployed no new land-based strategic missiles (ICBM) since 1969 (undertaking armament improvements for a portion of the Minuteman Force); the Soviets, since 1972, have deployed 12 variants of three highly-improved new systems involving over 800 new missiles and are already testing two more new types.

• The United States destroyed its biological warfare stocks in 1969; the Soviets greatly expanded production, with its proxies employing toxins against tribesmen in three countries in Asia.

• The total numbers of nuclear weapons in the U.S. stockpile has been reduced by 30 percent since the mid-sixties; the Soviet stockpile has skyrocketed.

• In 1980, the U.S. removed over 1,000 shorter-range nuclear weapons in Europe; the Soviets have steadily increased their shorter-range weaponry.

3. *Historical Assumptions:* The facts suggest to these evangelicals that the Soviets are determined militarists with an eschatology of victory. Defections to the Strong Deterrence school by formerly "dovish" liberals like Norman Podhoretz, editor of *Commentary* magazine, have

added new credibility to a strong critique of Soviet policies. These evangelicals would say this is not a new Cold War as much as it is a recognition of the inhumane and militant character of the Soviet Socialist State.

The Moral Deterrent school would agree with President Carter's Defense Secretary Harold Brown when he said, "When we build, they build; when we stop building, they build." Unlike some secular pragmatic defenders, the Moral Deterrent group does not call for drastic nuclear build-up. The Soviets are ruthlessly pragmatic, and a massive rearmament along MAD lines would be destabilizing. Ironically, many Moral Defense proponents oppose the nuclear freeze because it too would "freeze us into MAD" by disallowing changes in defense technology.

4. *Distinctive Moral Deterrent Positions:*

• *Pure Defense Proponents:* Evangelical Senator William Armstrong of Colorado, along with President Reagan, is in the forefront of a heated debate over development of anti-weapon defense systems. Sometimes called High Frontier Defense, this view suggests that Mutual Assured Destruction must be replaced as the prevailing nuclear strategy. They stress that the targeting of weapons must replace the targeting of populations. The short-term plan involves readily-available non-nuclear, low-cost missiles arrayed near strategic sites in the U.S. The next stages would involve space-based, non-nuclear weapons. Such development of defense systems would be disallowed if the Nuclear Freeze Resolution was passed.

• *Counter-Force Proponents:* With the development of increasingly sophisticated technologies, large nuclear weapons are rapidly becoming obsolete. The counter-force defense would be a conscious shifting of targets from cities to military sites in an attempt to minimize threats to non-combatants. The acts of hard-nosed Soviet strategists may be more effectively deterred, say the counter-force proponents, by the threat of a low-power, highly accurate weapon which they think might be used than by the mere possession of weapons so devastating that we would never use them.

5. The Moral Deterrent proponents tend to be strong supporters of arms reduction negotiations. In particular, they have spoken in favor of the Reagan Administration's "Zero Option" arms proposal. That plan, proposed by the President to the Soviets, would eliminate on a global scale all intermediate-range nuclear missiles. Historically, the Soviets added new, powerful SS-20 missiles to their 19 force of over 600. The U.S. had frozen at zero any intermediate-range missiles and the Zero Option of the President would have kept the freeze in exchange for Soviet plans for dismantlement of its awe-inspiring force of over 600 missiles. Additionally, the President's proposal for START (Strategic Arms Reduction Talks) has been supported by this school of thought. START would bring nuclear arms reductions in two phases: (a) ballistic missile warheads equal to levels at least $1/3$ below current levels and up to $1/2$ on intercontinental missiles; (b) equal ceilings on other elements of strategic forces, including ballistic missile power. The Soviets have rebuffed the Administration on both proposals.

## The Moral Disarmament School

1. *Theological Assumptions:* The Moral Disarmament school is founded on the Anabaptist critique of the state in general and the relation of the Church to the state in particular. Drawing from the views of early church writers, these evangelicals are guided by a strong emphasis on the Sermon on the Mount in its broadest application. Governments, though possessing the sword, are ethically inferior when they must exercise threat and violence. Other methods of social ordering must be utilized, principally the

equal redistribution of resources, which would "disarm" many pockets of potential disenchantment (presently bringing hopelessness) and criminality (which is presumed to be primarily an expression of anomie or alienation). Nuclear arms, for the moral disarmamentist, are in themselves an evil manifestation of the "powers and principalities of darkness" that undergird many governments and, thus, must be repudiated.

2. *Strategic Assumptions:* The Moral Disarmament school stresses that the strategic nuclear forces of the United States and the Soviet Union will destroy our planet. A race has been in full swing since the 1940s and today the arsenals arrayed are said to be capable of producing a "nuclear winter." According to this view, the fact that no nuclear weapons have been used since World War II does not prove that deterrence can work. Rather, they say, it only proves that terror can stave off terror only for a time. Both sides have nuclear weapons and it is almost inevitable that we will use them unless we disarm. Once one weapon is used, all will be used. Limited nuclear war cannot exist. Disarmament, says the moral disarmamentist, is far more important than even our political liberty, because the existence of the human race is at stake.

3. *Historical Assumptions:* Drawing their analysis from revisionist historians of the Cold War, the Moral Disarmament school affixes substantial blame on the United States for the temper and pace of nuclear arms development. The Soviet Union is said to be a defensive power vis-a-vis the Western governments with "paranoia," not Marxist territorialism, fueling its actions.

The most effective political counselor to these evangelicals is Richard Barnet, the author of numerous books, including *The Alliance*. Barnet is a founder of the Institute for Policy Studies in Washington, D.C., a think tank which applies a strongly Marxist critique to strategic and political matters. His assistance to the Sojourners since the early 1970s and to Professor Ron Sider for the last decade has helped set a strong revisionist tone in the Moral Disarmament evangelical circles. The book, *The Fate of the Earth* by Jonathan Schell, has had a great impact on the Moral Disarmament school as well, adding his vision for a World Government. Additionally, Gandhi's influence has stimulated the Moral Disarmament school through the practical guidelines set out by Richard B. Gregg in *The Power of Nonviolence.*

4. *Distinctive Moral Disarmament Positions:*

• Absolute Moral Disarmament: Professor Ronald Sider, in his book, *Nuclear Holocaust and Christian Hope* (co-authored by Richard K. Taylor) creates a clear case for total disarmament. Sider presumes unilateral disarmament by the U.S. as an ultimate moral goal and describes an invasion by the Soviet Union. He then takes Gregg's *The Power of Nonviolence* and reworks it to form a concept called non-violent Civilian-Based Defense (CBD).

On the docks, Sider tells us, the invading army will be met by people bearing signs in the Russian language: "Don't shoot. We are your brothers and sisters"; "You are a child of God" and "Your life is precious." The CBD will dumbfound the Soviets by systematic non-collaboration, says Sider. The ethical presumption that undergirds Professor Sider's view is that coercive force is always evil. The individual is morally barred from self-defense and the state (the United States in this case) should similarly be restricted. Non-violence alone is rewarded by the Lord, except in certain "wars of liberation" against "oppressive structures." Anything less is submission to the "powers and principalities."

• Incremental Moral Disarmament: The Roman Catholic bishops' Statement on Nuclear Arms has stimulated much activity in the Moral Disarmament school. Like the bishops, some evangelicals believe that nuclear arms, because of their destructive power, make the just war argument obsolete. While admitting that nuclear deterrence has worked for 30 years, the incremental moral disarmamentists view nuclear weapons themselves as evil. Thus, not only is their use ethically prohibited, but also their possession and production. Logically, the incrementalist is a "nuclear pacifist" and urges nuclear disarmament by the United States as an act of ethical courage. Here, a variety of views of Soviet intentions and likely reactions comes into play and nuclear pacifists, from Rev. John R. W. Stott to Dr. Myron Augsburger of Washington Community Fellowship, differ on the details of the form, speed and extent of United States nuclear disarmament.

• The Moral Disarmament school strongly supports the Hatfield-Kennedy Nuclear Arms Freeze and other similar initiatives. This arms initiative is based upon the assumption that the United States and the Soviets are at parity, present overkill is beyond reason, on-site inspections are not necessary for verification and nuclear deterrence is fundamentally immoral.

## A BIBLICAL VIEW OF DEFENSE

This chapter is only intended to be a cursory summary of views. Evangelicals are far from homogeneous on nuclear arms issues and few matters can raise a ruckus like defense. But the possibility of real political effect in our time demands that we take the Word and each other seriously and work through the details of a biblical view of defense.

Certain serious tensions are present in the Moral Disarmament position which must be examined. The disarmamentists generally caricature deterrence as "nuclear idolatry," suggesting that the ultimate concern which drives people is often the "security" of nuclear arms. One difficulty with this view lies with the fact that most people, particularly evangelicals, do not "place their faith in weapons." The argument is terribly weakened because little attention is paid specifically to nuclear arms. If anything, people of the deterrence school, who often have sobering data at their fingertips, know clearly that the nuclear stalemate could only have been sustained without a holocaust through the grace and sovereignty of the Lord of All. Studying the details and fine points of strategic matters usually only heightens this sense of dependence. Thus, the phrase, "they place their faith in weapons" is not only inaccurate and somewhat meaningless in a logical sense, it is also destructive of honest communication.

The moral disarmamentists are also torn by their urge toward the absolutist position. In their most honest moments, the incrementalists must admit that most conventional weaponry would not fit their moral criteria. Thus, increasingly there appears to be a convergence toward the goal of absolutist disarmament. Briefly stated, if nuclear weapons are evil due to their disproportionate destructiveness, then many conventional weapons should also be renounced.

There is a great difficulty at this point: How much disarmament is "enough"? The Moral Disarmament school is now occupied by the subtle issue of the legitimacy of violence through "Wars of Liberation" in the developing world. If one presumes, as many moral disarmamentists do, that "justice" is revealed in redistribution from the haves to the have-nots in the world and in each nation, then the question of the morality of violence by the "oppressed classes" against the "ruling classes" is critical. Because economic redistribution of resources by the state is a primary ethical and political goal of many moral disarmamentists, governments must be formed which will carry out this view of justice. If existing governments refuse to appropriately carry out this mandate, they can be characterized as oppressive and therefore, illegitimate. If they are determined to be illegitimate, then revolutionary forces are said to possess the right to "wage peace." For a traditional pacifist, even this violence (which might result in the desired redistributional society) is ethically suspect. For the nonpurists, nuclear violence is obviously evil; the lines of other more politically agreeable forms of violence are more blurred. As a matter of fact, some forms of violence may actually be a form of "peace"-making.

Jack London, viewing the horrors of the Nazi and Stalin regimes of the thirties and forties, once defined history as "the hobnailed boot of a soldier stomping on a human face . . . forever." Evangelicals know that ultimately, London will be proven wrong. There is the terrible possibility, however, that we will be mesmerized by an illusory view of the militaristic Soviet Union and find ourselves in an immense Gulag. Such a monstrosity (which Ron Sider paints as at least a possibility after disarming) cannot in any way be considered an elevated ethic of true love. Rather, it would be the fruit of ethical inhumaneness on a scale that would make cruel King Herod wince.

## Suggestions for Action

• Pray regularly with like-minded people that evil be restrained in the Soviet Union, the U.S. and all nations so that righteousness would abound and grow.

• Join with five people in your local church and determine together to thoroughly analyze the Biblical responsibilities of government. Draw some conclusions about defense and its role in sustaining justice or its illegitimacy in the process of justice.

• Write your Senators and Congressmen asking them for information on the history of American and Soviet nuclear arms development. Ask them how they view

President Kennedy's strategy of mutual assured destruction.

• Thoroughly analyze your view of when, or if, legitimate violence or threat of violence can be used with scriptural support.

---

## Study Questions

1. Define the elements of peace as shown in the Scriptures. To what degree is this biblical reality capable of being manifested in your life? Your community? Your nation? The world?

2. Define the elements of peace from the Soviet perspective.

3. What is mutual assured destruction? Is it a theory or a strategic policy?

4. Does a legitimately established government have the right to defend its citizens? If so, under what principles? If not, what is the basis for non-defense or limited defense?

5. Study Romans 13 and cross reference the words "minister" and "servant" of God. Where else do you find these words? What are the implications for governments? By what criteria are they to be judged eternally?

6. Is the possession of nuclear weapons evil per se? Is the use of nuclear weapons of any kind evil per se? Is the threat to use nuclear weapons evil per se?

7. Analyze this set of propositions and the conclusion. Do they logically hold together?

   • Nuclear weapons are a development of evil.
   • The use of nuclear weapons is therefore evil.

- The threat to use nuclear weapons is consequently evil as well.

Therefore, the possession of nuclear weapons is evil and the only moral step that can logically be taken is unilateral disarmament.

## Suggested Readings

Woolsey, R. James, Editor. *Nuclear Arms: Ethics, Strategy, Politics.* San Francisco: Institute for Contemporary Studies, 1984. Woolsey is a former advisor to SALT Negotiations and many fine points are raised.

Lefever, Ernest, Editor. *The Apocalyptic Premise.* Washington, D.C.: Ethics and Pubic Policy Center, 1983. An excellent compendium of articles by authors of every opinion regarding nuclear arms.

Weigal, George. *The Peace Bishops.* Chicago: World Without War, 1982. This small pamphlet, written by a Roman Catholic, presents some of the subtle questions that must be asked in determining the best methods for securing peace in the nuclear age.

Novak, Michael. *Moral Clarity in the Nuclear Age.* Nashville: Thomas Nelson Publishing, 1983. A detailed presentation of the classical Christian tradition of the just war as it applies to nuclear arms.

Bernbaum, John, Editor. *Perspectives on Peacemaking.* Ventura, CA: Regal Books, 1984. These are the transcripts of the Pasadena Conference on Peacemaking in 1983. It is most effective as a clear, concise presentation of the moral disarmament school's theology, both from the absolutist disarmament perspective of Sider and Wallis and the incremental disarmament perspective of Rev. Stott, Dr. Bernbaum and others.

Graham, Daniel. *High Frontier:* A New National Strategy. New York: Pinnacle Books, 1983. This is a popular overview of the anti-MAD deterrent defense.

## About the Author

Charles W. Jarvis is the Legislative Director for U.S. Senator Charles E. Grassley, and has served as the legal advisor for the Cuban-Haitian Refugee Task Force of the Departments of State and Justice. He has degrees in Soviet-U.S. Relations and History from the University of Virginia and holds the Juris Doctor in International Law from George Mason University.

# PART II

## A PLAN FOR ACTION
## Tips on How the System Works
by
Richard Cizik
Research Director
National Association of Evangelicals

**About the Author**

Richard Cizik is director of legislative research for the National Association of Evangelicals. He holds degrees from Whitworth College and Denver Theological Seminary and has taken graduate courses at George Washington University. He has also held numerous political posts and has been a candidate for office in the state of Washington. Mr. Cizik and his wife, Virginia, reside in the Washington, D.C. area.

# 9
# ONE PERSON CAN MAKE A DIFFERENCE

In his Gettysburg Address, Abraham Lincoln raised a question about the United States that remains to be answered: " . . . whether that nation, or any nation so conceived and so dedicated, can long endure." From a Christian point of view, the most severe implications of this question are in the sphere of spiritual values.

It is evident that our nation is on a slippery slope of moral and spiritual decline. Most Christians are probably deeply concerned about this deterioration. They should be. On the other hand, too many of those who grieve over this state of affairs are doing nothing to change it. They thus become part of the problem.

Many have bought the old bromides that "one person can't make a difference" or "you can't fight city hall." You would think they could cite chapter and verse from some sacred text of American politics to support the assumptions. But they can't, because these clichés are dead wrong.

One person can make a difference. You can fight city hall! Or the White House! Or Congress! That fact is obvious experientially to those who have battled for social change. It should be clear theologically, because "with God all things are possible" (Matt. 19:26).

How do astute Christians influence legislation or administrative action and thereby literally help shape the course of history?

Few citizens have the time, inclination or the opportunity to become thoroughly familiar with every aspect of the political process. Fortunately for the nation, and for those of us who take their moral guidance from the Scriptures, this is not necessary. For while organic chemists may tell us quite a bit about the physical composition of food, grandma's less sophisticated knowledge still produced a good stew. So also can we succeed in the public arena if we have only the basic ingredients and follow the procedure for combining them.

Mastering the information contained in this section will not automatically bring about change, but you will find here the specific helps many newcomers to the world of politics need in order to get started. Christ told His followers that we were to "render therefore unto Caesar the things which are Caesar's and unto God the things that are God's" (Matt. 22:21). In a representative democracy, we the people ultimately are "Caesar." And as such we have a duty as the followers of Christ to establish a God-centered relationship to human government. This implies that we can no more reject participation in politics than we can divest ourselves of our skin. It means that we must learn the paths and pitfalls of our governmental system.

Others whose ambitions start and end in this world have already learned how to "work the system" on Capitol Hill or in local politics. It was of them that Christ observed, "The children of this world are in their generation wiser than the children of light" (Luke 16:8). Yet Christ also commanded His followers to "be wise as serpents and innocent as doves" (Matt. 10:16, *RSV*). Hopefully, the information in this section will assist the followers of Christ in securing the kind of wisdom our Lord recommended.

# 10
# UNDERSTANDING CONGRESS

Our American system of government is probably the most complicated on earth. It is also one of the most interesting, and—because the United States exerts world leadership—one of the most important. Because it is complicated, our system is a mystery to most U.S. citizens. If we are to work through it, however, it is important that we understand it and know how we can influence it for ethical concerns.

When the man on the street is queried as to the kind of government we have, he invariably responds, "A democracy, of course." To define democracy is no easy task. Democracy is both a set of values and a system of government. As a set of values, democracy nourishes a tolerance for differing ideas, a respect for minority rights and a concern for the individual that we consider essential in a decent and ordered society. As a system of government, democracy allows all enfranchised citizens to come together to discuss and pass laws. The word itself is made up of two Greek roots—*demos,* "the people," and *kratia,* "authority,"—and was used by the Greeks to mean government by the many, as contrasted with government by the few (oligarchy) or by one (autocracy).

Government "by the many," however, is not literally possible except in the simplest of societies. The day-by-day operation of government in modern nations must be in the hands of a small group of people. A democracy then is essentially a device to determine which of many competing groups shall run the government.

Fortunately, our Constitution has spelled out exactly how our government must respond to the many claims upon it by these competing groups. Our nation's founding fathers set up two devices to achieve their goals of preventing public officials from abusing their power and of preventing any one group of people, even a majority, from capturing control of the government and tyrannizing the rest of the people. These devices are: (1) an elaborate system of balancing power, so that government power is distributed among the three branches of the national government: the Executive (President), Legislative (Congress) and the Judiciary (Supreme Court); and (2) free and fair elections, so no one can take elective office without acceptance by a majority of the voters. Understanding these two devices is essential to having an impact on our nation, and thus the course of history.

Most Americans take for granted our system of separation of powers. The separating and checking of power seems to be the essence of constitutional government. But this balance of power does not come naturally. Our Constitution had to stipulate it. While it grants the president broad executive authority by vesting in the presidency the executive power of the United States, it gives to Congress the legislative power: "All legislative power herein shall be vested in Congress of the United States, which shall consist of a Senate and a House of Representatives." These powers and the organization of Congress are further defined in Article I of the Constitution. They include, for example, that the Senate and the House of Representatives are chosen by direct election. There are two senators from each state with one third of the total Senate body elected every two years for six-year terms. The federal census determines each state's portion of 435 representative seats, so that every citizen has one representative in the House of Representatives. State legislatures determine congressional district boundaries, with every state allowed at least one representative. All representatives are elected for two-year terms.

Since Congress is the seat of legislative authority and one of the main channels for citizen input, it deserves the focus of our attention. Moreover, few people can deal directly with either a president or a Supreme Court. But any person can communicate with his elected representatives in Washington.

Unfortunately, ignorance of Congress and disinterest in its activities are widespread. Surveys have revealed that most voters do not know even the names of their representative or two senators. Scarcely a majority of voters even know whether the Democrats or Republicans control Congress, and hence much of the electorate is not in a very good position to hold either party accountable for its performance on Capitol Hill.

Just what should be known about Congress? A foreign observer once joked that "Congress is so strange. A man gets up to speak and says nothing. Nobody listens—and then everybody disagrees." Actually, the work of Congress is quite serious. And whether we like it or not, Congress is an integral part of our lives. Just accept this fact. Good, bad or in between, Congress affects what we do and what we may not do, how well we live, how warm our houses will be in the winter, how cool in the summer and how we will get to our offices, schools, or shopping centers.

We may not like some of what Congress does, but the laws that emanate from it create—or reflect—the beliefs and climate of our lives: in our work, our leisure, and ultimately our survival. So nearly everything Congress does has an impact and we need to pay attention to it.

The Constitution is explicit about the powers of Congress. In addition to writing federal laws, Congress has the power to conduct investigations, monitor federal agencies, impeach federal officials including the president and declare war. It has the power to approve treaties and all top federal agency and judicial appointments as well as armed forces officer appointments. Congress also helps to shape public opinion and exercise the power of legislative oversight—that is, it keeps an eye on what the Executive branch does. It also has power to raise or lower federal taxes and appropriate money to run the government.

## HOW CONGRESS WORKS

Most of us picture Congress as a solemn deliberative body which sets national policy after deep reflection and careful debates. We think of the great debates in the past between such political legends as Henry Clay and Daniel Webster. Today, however, the business of Congress can be summed up as the superintending of a large, expensive and complex federal government. The occasions for making sweeping policy decisions are relatively few.

Most of the work of Congress is done in committees and subcommittees. The committees are, as a Speaker of the House once said, "The eyes, the ears, the hands, and very often the brain of the House." The reasons for this are fairly obvious. Without some division of labor the volume of business confronting Congress would be overwhelming. Congress has responded to this pressure by delegating work to these "little legislatures."

While it is not true that committees decide everything

and that other aspects of Congress are mere window
dressing, there is no question but that legislative measures receive their most severe scrutiny in committees
and that the outlines of all legislation as well as the details
of most initiatives are settled in committees or subcommittees. What happens in committees must then necessarily be of concern to those interested in influencing Congress.

There are four types of Congressional committees: (1)
Special or select committees ordinarily make specific
investigations rather than introduce legislation. After sub-
mitting their report they are dissolved. (2) When problems
rise that need joint consideration, the House and Senate
occasionally create joint committees composed of members of both chambers. (3) Conference committees, a special kind of joint committee, are appointed by the officers
of the House and Senate when the two chambers disagree
over legislation. (4) By far the most important are the
standing committees. They number 22 in the House and
16 in the Senate and are divided into over one-hundred
subcommittees in each chamber. These committees have
great power, because all bills introduced in the House and
Senate are referred to them. They can defeat bills,
pigeonhole them for weeks, amend them beyond recognition or speed them on their way. Among the most important of these House Standing Committees are the spending and taxing committees—namely, Appropriations,
Ways and Means and the Rules Committee. Among the
most important Senate Committees are Foreign Relations, Finance, Appropriations and Government Operations.

## HOW A BILL BECOMES A LAW
Once a bill has been introduced in either the House or
the Senate, the parliamentarian or leadership of whichever

body receives the bill refers it to a committee where the chair and staff determine what subcommittee, if any, is to receive it. If a bill is going to die, it usually does so at the committee or subcommittee level. Whether by research, debate, hearing testimony or markup (the actual revising of the final draft of legislation), committee action is critical.

Subcommittees have become increasingly important in recent years; they have proliferated to the point where there are several hundred. The nitty-gritty work—not just drafting legislation, but understanding of what is going on in government—takes place mostly in subcommittee. Committees, with their large memberships, tend to ratify subcommittees' decisions or at least to accept the structuring of the debate as it comes from subcommittee.

But not all subcommittees are equal. In the House, some are far more important than others. There are perhaps a dozen or so very important subcommittees. And it is here that the largest percentage of legislating takes place. Chairmen, elected by their committee members, count their votes very carefully and keep in close touch with their colleagues. While actions in subcommittees may appear obscure, it is not beyond the ingenuity of the interested citizen to understand them. And, fortunately, Congress is very responsive, with "hair-trigger" accuracy, to the views of the voting public.

Citizen input is valuable at two junctures in the committee process. One such time is before the scheduling of hearings on bills. Constituent requests for full and respectful hearings on a bill often cause committee staff to schedule hearings. Most bills are not considered at all. For instance, over the past 14 years, an average of more than 20,000 bills has been introduced in the House of Representatives during each two-year term. Only slightly more than 10 percent have even been reported from committees to the House floor. And, of the 20,000 introduced, the average number that became law per Congress is under 5 percent.

Another occasion for citizen input is during the committee consideration of the bill. Letters of concern to one's own congressman on the appropriate committee or subcommittee will often make a difference in the outcome. To do this, however, necessitates that we know the respective committees and subcommittees on which our representatives or senator(s) serve. The names of subcommittee members can be found in the *Congressional Directory, The Congressional Yellow Pages* or in other directories published by various interest groups.

If a majority of the subcommittee approves, the bill goes back to the full committee where it again must be approved by majority vote before it goes to the House or Senate floor. Agreement within the committee on the contents of a bill does not mean agreement in Congress when the bill reaches the full House or Senate floor. Sometimes the same parts of the bill stricken by the committee are included, or whole new portions are suggested. The full House or Senate may vote for or against a bill, or change the measure and then approve it.

Another key time to contact your legislators is just before the bill is about to come up for a vote in the full House or Senate. You should contact both your senators if it is a Senate bill and your representative if it is a House bill. If the House or Senate passes the bill it then is moved to the other chamber where it is referred to a committee. Again, it goes to the floor if a majority of the committee approves. Approval of the floor means both the House and Senate have separately cleared the bill.

Even after both Houses of Congress have passed a bill, still more changes may occur. Usually the House and Senate don't pass identical versions of the bill. So the bill must go to a joint conference committee, which comes up with a final version satisfactory to both houses.

After coming all this way the bill goes to the president, who can either veto it or sign it into law. Because of all these and other possible delays, changes and compromises, it may be necessary to write letters on the same piece of legislation a number of times.

As complicated as this all sounds, Congress does work for and is responsive to the electorate. Admittedly, it gets pressure from all sides. One member of Congress has indicated that it takes just that—pressure from all sides—to keep it upright. For that reason in particular Congress needs to hear the ethical concerns of Christians.

## FORMS OF CONGRESSIONAL ACTION

There are four forms under which the House and Senate act. They are the bill, the joint resolution, the concurrent resolution and the simple resolution. Bills are the most common form of congressional action.

For example, in the 97th congress (1980-82) there were 10,580 bills, 908 joint resolutions, 575 concurrent resolutions, and 1,172 simple resolutions introduced. Of these only 473 became public law. A bill or resolution number indicates only the order in which it was introduced into the House or Senate. A bill or resolution will often be informally referred to by the name of its chief sponsor.

*Bills:* House bills are headed H.R., followed by a number. H.R. stands for House of Representatives, not House Resolution. Senate bills are headed S., followed by a number. Bills are used for general legislation. Any type of public bill may originate in either the House or the Senate, except bills raising revenue which must originate in the House.

*Joint Resolutions:* A joint resolution is styled H.J.Res. or S.J.Res., followed by a number. Bills and joint resolutions are used interchangeably except in the case of pro-

# How a Bill Becomes Law

This graphic shows the most typical way in which proposed legislation is enacted into law. There are more complicated, as well as simpler, routes, and most bills fall by the wayside and never become law.

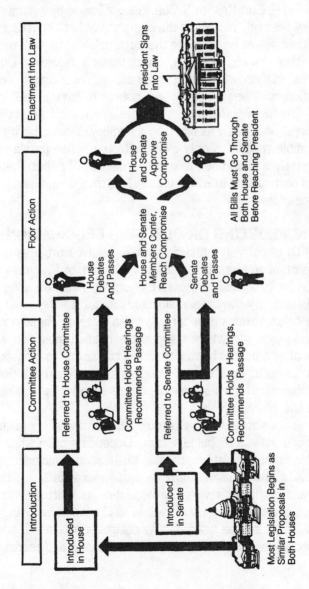

posed constitutional amendments which are written as joint resolutions.

*Concurrent Resolutions:* A concurrent resolution is headed H. Con. Res. or S. Con. Res., followed by a number. They normally pertain to the operation of both houses and by themselves do not have the force of law. They are used to express facts, opinions, principles or a "sense of Congress" statement directed to the nation. A concurrent resolution must be passed by both houses to have any effect.

*Simple Resolution:* A simple resolution is styled H. Res. or S. Res., followed by a number. The authority of a simple resolution only extends to the house passing it. They have been used to express the will of either House on a particular matter. By themselves they do not have the force of law.

## SUPPORTING OR OPPOSING LEGISLATION

To effectively influence our legislative process it is important to learn that getting a member of Congress to vote for or against a measure is only a minimum level of influence. By the time a bill comes up for a vote, most of the controversies have already been settled. Those occasions when a legislator's support is needed most are: (1) just after a bill has been introduced and needs cosponsors, (2) during committee decision-making, (3) on the floor during debates when opponents are introducing weakening amendments.

A constituent can exercise real influence by urging specific actions by his legislator. Depending upon where a bill is in the legislative process, these actions include:

*Ask your congressman to cosponsor a bill.* All this means is that he favors the legislation as written, with a clear understanding that it will in all likelihood be changed during committee hearings. By cosigning onto a bill, however, a legislator is influencing his colleagues and sending a message to the committee it has been assigned to that it has broad support.

*Ask your congressman to request hearings on a bill.* Such a request is directed to the chairman of the committee to which the bill has been assigned, since he controls the agenda. While sending a letter of this sort is officially done by the sponsor of the bill, additional letters often are necessary to get hearings. As stated earlier, most bills never get out of committee. Some committees, such as the House Judiciary Committee, are known for being "graveyards" for certain legislative proposals. Conversely, a letter to the chairman opposing hearings on a measure is equally effective.

*Once hearings are over, ask your congressman to urge the committee to report out the bill.* Just because a committee has held hearings doesn't mean that it has to take any action. Many bills fade into oblivion after hearings never to be seen again. If you oppose a bill that has received hearings, ask your legislator to urge the chairman and committee members to reject the bill.

*When the bill is on the floor, ask your congressman to speak to other legislators urging their support of a bill* without weakening amendments. A request that he make a speech from the floor of the chamber is certainly appropriate. And, of course, a similar request to make a speech of opposition is relevant if you oppose the bill.

*And, of course, ask your congressman to vote for a bill.* If you oppose a piece of legislation, don't be afraid to ask for a negative vote.

## Suggested Readings

The following is a list of books that will help you find the information you need about Congress and gain an insider's viewpoint on the Senate and House of Representatives. These are books of general value to you in planning your efforts to influence legislators. Other books useful in more specific ways are listed in bibliographies following each of the chapters in this book.

## Directories

Barone, Michael; Ujifusa, Grant and Matthews, Douglas. *The Almanac of American Politics.* New York: E.P. Dutton, 1978. Revised every two years. This is the best all-around directory of legislators in Congress. It contains a brief and perceptive analysis of the political situation in each state and congressional district, and also includes voting records, congressional district maps, and committee lists.

*Congressional Directory.* Published in odd-numbered years; a supplement is published in alternate years. Available from Superintendent of Documents, Washington, D.C. 20402. The little-noted but useful contents of this directory include a list of all news media personnel accredited to the House and Senate, and seniority rankings of all members of Congress.

Brownson, Charles B. *Congressional Staff Directory* Published annually. Available postpaid from Congressional Staff Directory, P.O. Box 62, Mount Vernon, VA 22121. Lists all members of a legislator's staff with their titles. Also covers committee staff and contains capsule biographies of many staffers. Because it provides basic data on legislators too, it can be used as an all-purpose directory when you're dealing with a large number of legislators. However, it's not worth the price if your efforts concern only a handful of legislators.

*Legislative Directory.* Published annually. Available postpaid from American Gas Association, 1515 Wilson Boulevard, Arlington, VA 22209. The best inexpensive, pocket-sized directory of Congress, containing the basic data on each legislator, with congressional district maps and the names of the administrative assistant and the legislative assistant who handles energy issues.

## Legislators Look at Congress

Tacheron, Donald G. and Udall, Morris. *The Job of the Congressman.* Indianapolis: The Bobbs-Merrill Co., 1970. Second edition. A how-to-do-it book for new members of the House of Representatives. Has become the standard text for all newcomers to Capitol Hill, legislators, staffers, and lobbyists alike. Also contains a good bibliography of political science books about Congress.

Riegle, Donald W., Jr. with Armbrister, Trevor. *O Congress.* New York: Popular Library, 1976. Based on a year of Riegle's diary while he was a congressman from Michigan. He describes the frustrations of a young congressman, trying to influence legislation in the House, keep his supporters happy back home and maintain a life of his own.

## Political Science

Redman, Eric. *The Dance of Legislation.* New York: Simon & Schuster, 1973. Redman, a former aide to Senator Warren Magnuson tells the story of the drafting and enactment of the National Health Service Corps bill, of which Magnuson was a lead sponsor.

Harris, Joseph P. *Congress and the Legislative Process.* New York: McGraw Hill, 1972. A standard textbook for a neophyte to the political process. In a sensible and readable fashion, the book describes how our laws are made.

Peters, Charles. *How Washington Really Works.* Addison and Wesley, 1980. Peters exposes the Washington that only "insiders" know about. Subjects covered include the presidency, congress, the press, lobbies and other governmental institutions.

# 11

# UNDERSTANDING POLITICAL PARTIES

The specter of certain evangelical Christians tossing their hats into the political ring has received considerable attention. This development, however, is far from characteristic of the evangelical community as a whole. Most are not even living up to their responsibilities as individual citizens. (See data in elections section.) In this respect, we are not much different from the rest of society. Most citizens are not interested in playing even a small policy making role. They do not join interest groups, volunteer for party work, communicate with their representatives or talk politics with their friends, except in a vague or uninformed way. As one pundit put it: "Applause, mingled with boos and hisses, is about all the average voter is willing to contribute to public life."

One explanation for this lack of participation in the political process is that people do not understand it. If you want to play baseball or tennis or engage in any sport, you must learn the rules, and go where the sport is played. It's also necessary to equip yourself with the tools of the game. If you don't understand the sport, some of the players' actions may not make sense. Even after you learn to play you may not agree with all the rules, but if you want to play, you must adapt to them. So it is with politics. While our nation's governmental system is not perfect it is preferable to all others. If Christians are to have a voice in it, it's up to them to learn how the system functions.

## HOW THE PARTIES FUNCTION

Short of running for political office those who get involved in political parties will have the greatest degree of influence upon the political system. The reasons for this arise from what political parties are and the roles that they perform.

Just what is a political party? The typical response to such a question is "Democrats and Republicans, of course." And this is correct. We do have these two major political parties in our country. But every definition of a political party depends on the different aspects one sees. In general, a political party can be defined as a group of people organized and operating to secure control of a government, state, or country. It is comprised of: (1) an inner circle of people who are either office-holders or office-seekers, (2) a network of party leaders, (3) party activists at the grassroots who give time and money, in addition to votes, to the party's candidates, and (4) voters who identify with the party, and almost always support its candidates.

And what does a political party do? More than any other force, the political party tends to keep the wheels of government in a democracy turning. There is always the danger that government, confronted with the enormity of the tasks it is expected to perform, and with conflicting judgments as to the best way ahead, will become ineffective. Moreover, government is a great leviathan, and without the tension that political parties create, its sheer size

**Typical State**

**POLITICAL PARTY STRUCTURE**

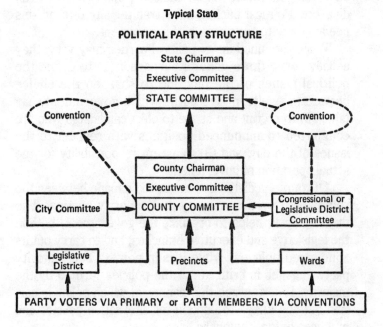

and strength would render it ineffectual.

So, unless these conflicting interests in society can be united upon some basis to allow for effective governmental action, the result will be deadlock, impotence or even disaster. Political parties have traditionally offered this needed unity to the process of government.

While the functions of political parties may vary, they usually serve three general purposes: (1) to define the political issues of the day and to sharpen the choice between the alternative paths which government may take, (2) to recruit and strive to elect candidates who are committed to announced positions with respect to the issues of the day, and (3) to accept responsibility for the actual operation of government.

Of course, a distinction needs to be made between the role played by the majority and minority parties. The majority party helps to organize the government, both in the legislative and executive branches, and to carry out its announced policies, while it is in power. The minority party engages in criticism of the policies formed by the majority. It scrutinizes the manner in which policy is carried out and keeps the option for alternative policies and practices before the public.

Although in practice our parties often fail to perform all of these functions, these roles still stand in theory. The organization of party machinery closely parallels the two main roles of the party: winning elections and running the government. On paper the party is organized like an army. It resembles in form a pyramid. Millions of party members and thousands of local party leaders and followers comprise this pyramid. The problem with this analogy is that, unlike an army, the parties are very decentralized and without discipline. Nonetheless, the traditional party organization, is at least hierarchical in form and parallels the various levels of government—local, state and national.

At each level the party machinery usually consists of a nominating convention (or caucus) at the base, a central committee in the middle and a chairman at the top.

## Party Machinery

The nominating convention is made up of delegates who are selected in varying ways and represent the rank and file of party members. The conventions meet in election years to determine party policies through the selection of a platform in which the party takes a stand on the issues. And, most importantly, the convention selects the party's nominees for public office where that is not done through a primary election.

At the national level, the party convention meets every four years to nominate presidential and vice-presidential candidates. It writes the platform, adopts rules and formalizes the election of a national committee. But apart from these functions, the convention has little authority. At the state and local levels, the nomination process may include a state convention, county conventions, congressional district conventions and local party meetings called caucuses. Delegates for these conventions are selected by the local party.

The second structure in the party organization is the central committee. It is a smaller entity, usually selected at conventions and serves as the party's governing body between conventions. Heading this committee is a chairman, who is the top executive officer of the party. At the national level, in addition to serving as the party's governing body, the committee offers advice, helps during the campaign and selects the site of the national convention. It is comprised of two members from each state who are selected by the party at the state level.

At the state level, the central committee conducts the party's business, such as directing state campaigns, operating party headquarters, organizing party fundraising and convening official party functions. At the local level, there is usually a county as well as a town or city central committee. The county committee is charged with carrying the county for the party. It raises money, puts on voter registration drives and helps build a strong precinct organization. Membership in the county committee usually consists of party members elected by the various legislative districts and precincts within the county.

The city or town central committee is composed of precinct (captains) leaders who are elected by the registered voters of that party in their precinct. If the precincts are combined into wards for organizational purposes, the ward leader becomes a member in the party's town or city executive committee as well.

The precinct is the basic building block of the political parties. It is geographically drawn by election officials so as to have nearly equivalent voting population in each precinct. Each precinct leader is responsible for organizing his precinct and delivering the party vote on election day. The precincts often provide the margins of victory or defeat for the candidates through their efforts in meeting with voters, registering them to vote, distributing literature and then getting them out to vote. They are the "foot soldiers" of the political parties.

In fact, one incentive for many people to get involved in the parties is that most of the power rests in state and local organizations. Our national parties are simply loose alliances of state and local parties, joined together every four years for the purpose of winning a presidential election. This high degree of decentralization arises because of the size and diversity of our nation. People always think first of their local and sectional interests, and, following the path of least resistance, the parties reflect these interests. This makes for strong local party organizations. And these organizations are always seeking volunteers, particularly at the most important political unit—the local precinct. Thus, citizenship participation in government can begin right in your own neighborhood.

## GUIDELINES FOR VOLUNTEERING

Here are rules to follow when volunteering your help:

(1) Be a willing volunteer. Party politics used to be dominated by small cliques in each state and county, but it's not like that any more. Party leaders are always looking for willing volunteers. Moreover, if Christians leave opportunities for participation open and unfilled, the void will be filled by those who do not share a similar ethical concern. We must be careful not to lose by default what could be won with some additional effort on our part. The words of former Senator Sam Ervin dramatize the choice before us: "If men and women of capacity refuse to take part in politics and government, they condemn themselves, as well as the people, to the punishment of living under bad government."

(2) To get started, contact the local party headquarters and indicate your willingness to help. Ask when the next party meeting will be. Then attend and strike up conversations with some of the active people. You usually won't have to volunteer; you'll be asked to do something—perhaps to serve on a membership committee or to be a poll watcher in your precinct at the next election.

(3) If you've been active in the party, you might become a convention delegate. Get a friend to nominate you when delegates are being selected. As a delegate, you would have influence and your support would be courted by candidates for various nominations. Your stature as a delegate carries over into issue work as well, increasing your influence upon the issue stands the party takes.

Obviously those who volunteer their efforts and serve effectively and faithfully will soon rise to leadership and become those who determine issue stands and handpick the candidates.

(4) Recognize that your political involvement is an act of service and must be carried out with a humble attitude. This means being willing to be a servant.

(5) Perform your civic duties with the understanding that you can only do what you believe to be God's will. But be careful not to claim that your deeds constitute the will of God so others won't scoff and mock God. Indeed, one of the explanations why people have a negative attitude toward the mixing of Christianity and politics is that Christians have often attempted to use the power of government to impose "God's will" upon society.

(6) Neither is it appropriate to claim that we have the answers simply because we are Christians. Instead, approach each task with the belief that without God's grace we have no hope of finding out real solutions to society's difficult problems.

(7) Encourage others to join as volunteers for a party, but don't charge in with the intention of taking over or "throwing the rascals out." Remember that those who are in positions of influence have usually earned the right to exercise that influence. You'll have to earn the same right.

## 12

# COMMUNICATING EFFECTIVELY

### THE LETTER

One of the most frequently asked questions is "Do contacts with legislators make a difference?" A government official, a veteran of about 20 years on Capitol Hill, once said: "If the average member of Congress received as many as half a dozen letters scrawled in pencil on brown wrapping paper, it would be enough to change his vote on most issues." Perhaps he has exaggerated, but his remarks indicate that members of Congress want to know what their constituents are thinking.

A 1983 survey conducted by the *Washingtonian* magazine of 219 top congressional staffers confirms this. According to the survey, the most influential factors in the decision-making process of members of Congress were (in order of priority): (1) a member's political philosophy, (2) constituent opinion, (3) office mail, (4) the White House position, (5) party leaders, (6) press back home, (7) Washington lobbies, and (8) the national media.

These results reveal the importance placed on constituent thinking. Aside from a member's political philosophy, constituent opinion and office mail are more likely to determine his position on issues than even the position held by the White House or party leaders—proof that constituents are thus some of the most important people in a legislator's life.

The most important influence upon a congressman's voting behavior remains his ideological predisposition. His convictions will determine how he votes on a host of issues. Like anyone else, members of Congress indulge in selective perception and recall of what they hear. Most messages that a congressman hears or reads raise the prominence of a particular issue as much as they change attitudes on a subject. Letters force a member to think more about an issue and to become more prone to express whatever bias he has regarding it.

Messages from constituents serve more as triggers than as persuaders, unless the member's opinion is not yet formed. In that case, letters and phone calls from constituents become more influential in making the decision. Most congressional staffers agree that even one well written letter on a subject can start the staff thinking about that issue. These aides see each letter as representing the opinions of many people who do not write. A number of letters on the same topic may prompt the assignment of a staff member to draft a position-paper for the congressman. In some cases, a letter may actually change a legislator's mind, particularly when a member is wavering on an issue.

But whether or not a communication from a constituent is the determining factor in a member's voting behavior, it is not ignored. Members of Congress and administration officials—at least those who want to remain in Washington—are sensitive to the feelings and opinions of their constituents. The pros and cons are counted and the administrative assistant to a member of Congress regularly reports on the mail received. Telegrams sometimes go directly to the legislator's desk. Phone calls are also tallied and reported.

Communication with elected officials, therefore, should be regarded not only as a privilege of citizenship but also as a responsibility. Members of Congress respect and appreciate that communication. Even a letter disagreeing with an elected official's stated position is worthwhile, because it can help your representative to understand the other side of that issue. Do not become discouraged, however, if, following your literary effort, the member's vote is still unfavorable to your position. It is important to remember that other persuasive people have also contacted the member, and the next time the vote may go your way.

It is critical, though, that your message be presented as effectively as possible. On the first occasion, writing a letter to your congressman may seem difficult. But it can be done and done well. You do not need to be an expert on an issue to get attention. Neither do you need to be a literary wizard. Here are some basic rules to follow:

## 1. Concentrate on your own delegation.

Your two senators and your representative have an obligation to consider your views. Generally, as a courtesy, letters from outside a congressman's district are forwarded to the congressman from whose district it was sent. Of course, if a staffer doesn't have the time to do this, the letter will end up in the wastebasket.

## 2. Confine your letter to one specific legislative subject.

This ensures that it will be seen by the right staff member. To do otherwise is to decrease the force of your argument and complicate any response to it. Also, tell the legislator exactly what you want done.

### 3. Ask the legislator to tell you his position on the matter.

Will he support or oppose this legislation? He has a responsibility to inform you as to where he stands.

### 4. Write in your own words.

Mass produced letters that are part of a mail campaign or petition drive are of little influence. Form letters usually receive form replies. In other words, your congressman or his staff assistant will measure your interest in an issue by the amount of time you take to inform him of your beliefs. If you are willing to take only 30 seconds (the time it takes to sign a petition, postcard, or form letter) to protest your representative's action or inaction, he will conclude that you are really not serious about your concern. A two- or three-sentence personal letter has more impact than a preprinted postcard. This kind of seriousness is a measurement of your capacity to elect another representative.

### 5. Be brief.

Letters that are more than one page are saved for another day. Completeness and clarity are both possible on one page. It will take more effort to condense your ideas into a single page, but it's worth it if you want to be read. Letters need not be typed, but they must be legible.

### 6. Give your reasons for taking a stand.

But avoid emotional arguments or language that is demanding or threatening. While the subject may be emotion-laden, use facts and illustrations to make your point. Statements like "Vote against HR100, I'm bitterly opposed" do not help much. But a letter which says "I'm a small hardware dealer, and HR100 will put me out of business for the following reasons—" says much more. If you disagree with your legislator, say so but do not berate him. Try to keep the dialogue open. Your attitude will inevitably come through and it should be polite and positive. Displaying anger or resentment in a letter only makes it easier to ignore. Your legislator will only assume that you wouldn't vote for him even if he did what you ask, and you want him to think of you as a potential supporter.

## 7. Do not assume that your member is well informed about a given issue.

A member can't stay on top of everything. Treat him with respect, but do explain the situation.

## 8. Be constructive.

Indicate how a bill is counterproductive. Letters should, whenever possible, include the bill number or the popular title since there can be many bills concerning any given topic.

## 9. Ask for a response.

Request an answer to a specific question. A well-formulated question will often get a more personal response. Write a letter that cannot be answered by a computer.

## 10. Be timely.

Read the newspaper or institutional newsletters such as our own for dates of scheduled floor votes or committee action. Obviously, your letter should come as early as possible before decisions are made. By doing so it's possible to encourage the legislator to take the right position before the opposition gets to him. The best time to write is when you first learn that Congress is going to consider the issue.

## 11. Be accurate and courteous.

Be certain that your name and address are on both the envelope and letter. Write legibly and spell names accurately. Use proper etiquette. Any legislator is called "Honorable" on the envelope and inside address. The salutation, however, treats senators and representatives of the House differently. Representatives are addressed as "Mr.," "Ms." or "Mrs.," while senators are called "Senator."

## 12. Point out the moral issues involved.

Explain why you are for a particular position. Since legislators get so much mail from special interest groups, they need to hear from citizens who are primarily concerned with what seems right to them on moral grounds.

## 13. If you have expert knowledge, share it.

Of all the letters pouring into a congressman's office, perhaps one in a hundred comes from a constituent who is a real expert in that subject. All opinions expressed are important, but those from someone with real experience are a gold mine to conscientious members.

## 14. Say "well done" when deserved.

Your members of Congress are human, too, and appreciate a word of thanks from people who believe they have done the right thing. Thank your legislator if he voted for your position on an issue. Very few constituents bother to do this. It will be appreciated! Also, do this while the vote is still fresh in the congressman's mind. If possible, phone after a vote and leave a message of thanks.

## 15. Avoid becoming a constant "pen pal."

Quality, not quantity, is what counts. Write when you feel like it, but don't try to instruct your congressman on every issue that comes up. Writing only once a month is a good rule. One of the pet peeves on Capitol Hill is the "pen pal" who weighs down the mail every few days with long tomes on every conceivable subject.

## 16. Always keep copies of correspondence.

Retain and file a copy of your letter and the reply from your representative. They are especially useful should you arrange an interview to discuss your concerns.

## 17. Try to get together with others.

One final suggestion: Join with others, if possible, and write your individual letters in a group. There is motivation and support in numbers. If you've never written a letter to a legislator, hearing of someone else's experience can encourage you to try your own hand at it. If you receive a negative response, it helps to have others with whom to talk it over.

## THE FOLLOW-UP LETTER

Whatever the response, write a follow-up letter. If your congressman cannot comply with your request for legislative support, he may send back a letter agreeing with you on some other area of interest. Ignore this kind of flattery.

But if your legislator does disagree with you, write back promptly, refuting his arguments and once more asking him to take the position you favor. If you fail to follow up, the legislator and his staff will have little reason to reconsider his position. They will get the impression that either his letter persuaded you or that you didn't care strongly enough about the issue to pursue it further.

When follow-up letters arrive in a congressional office, the picture can change. These letters will communicate that the legislator's position is raising serious objections from constituents. Make these letters thoughtful and courteous, but insistent. This will require the staff to draft answers to your points.

Cover at least three elements in follow-up letters:

1. Express thanks for the legislator's candidness in stating his position.
2. Tell him you disagree and proceed to refute his arguments. Make new points, if you can.
3. Ask a question or two, so the staff will have to think about the issue and respond. Some suggested questions include: Have you consulted . . . ? Can you back up that question . . . ? Did you know . . . ?

Above all, do not get discouraged. Remember, your legislator needs your help in casting votes. The "ballot box" is not far away. It's painted red, white and blue, and it reads "U.S. Mail."

## TELEGRAMS AND MAILGRAMS

There is only one use for a telegram or mailgram and that is when it is too late for a letter. In most offices they are treated the same as a letter. In many instances, their value is less than that of a thoughtful letter since a telegram or a mailgram is usually too expensive to communicate the reasons for your support. Nonetheless, they are especially helpful to reemphasize your position just before the vote on a critical issue.

Telegrams are fast, but costly. Western Union will deliver a telegram of 10 words or less within two to five hours for $8.75; delivery by a messenger costs $17.70. Mailgrams have almost made telegrams obsolete. They provide next-day service by mail for a message of 50 words or less at only $7.50. Western Union also has available the "opinion gram." It provides same-day service to members of Congress using a telex system. A message of 20 words or less costs $4.50.

## TELEPHONE CALLS

You can also register your opinion by a telephone call, although this is usually only effective if the issue you are calling about is well known to your legislator. If you've not written a letter, a phone call will at least get you on record. Many constituents incorrectly assume that they must call the legislator's Washington office to register a viewpoint or talk about an issue. A call to the congressional district office is just as effective, especially if you can generate a large volume of calls. When you call the local office indicate that you want to register a citizen opinion or talk briefly with a staff member who is handling a particular issue. Briefly state your position and ask for a reply from the congressman.

When calls come into the local office, the Washington office is informed. Since most people are too apathetic to make a call, a dozen or more calls to the local offices can really make a difference. Staff in the district office are usually more politically oriented, and very sensitive to what constituents are thinking.

A number of cautions about phone usage are in order. If you do use the phone to talk to staffers about an issue, avoid overdoing it. The constituent who calls once or twice a week to chat about issues can become annoying to staffers who are trying to handle their normal heavy work load.

Don't forget: your communication counts!

# 13

# UNDERSTANDING ELECTIONS AND VOTING INTELLIGENTLY

Every election year two questions are put to adult Americans: "Will you vote?" and "Who will you vote for?" How we answer these questions is very important. Unfortunately, many of us have chosen not to vote. Just why we do not vote is worth a serious look. Understanding why is the first step to changing it. Who we vote for is also critical. The candidates selected make an impression and apparently determine whether or not many choose to vote the next time.

## ASKING WHY

Why do millions of citizens choose not to vote? There are basically two theories. The most popular view is that there is a profound crisis of confidence in the U.S. political process. Historian George MacGregor Burns asserts that "Americans are no longer merely criticizing their political system, they are deserting it." In his view this is because voters "see no choice between the parties and no longer expect leaders to live up to their promises."

There is some evidence to support this view. A 1983 survey conducted by ABC-TV found that nonvoters, much more than voters, believe elections make no difference and that individuals do not influence policy.

The second probable cause for low voter turnout is the difficulty of registration requirements and voting procedures. There is evidence to support this thesis. A University of California study reported in a public opinion magazine shows that 85 percent of Americans say they are proud of our political institutions. So why then the low voter turnout? Registration deadlines in the U.S. are often as obscure as the procedures themselves. Moreover, every time a person moves, it's necessary to register all over again. On top of this, the burden of registration in the U.S. falls on the individual rather than the government. The opposite is true in most other democracies.

To test the hypothesis that registration difficulties contribute to low voter turnout, a survey was done of those states that put up the fewest obstacles to voting. In those states that allow election-day registration (Maine, Minnesota, Oregon and Wisconsin) the voter turnout ranged from a low of 61 percent to a high of 70 percent. These results were all better than the national average of 52 percent.

If there is any conclusion to be drawn from these results, it is that voter participation will probably continue to remain low until registration procedures are changed. Since this is unlikely, the best solution is to help educate voters in registration requirements.

In all likelihood then, the explanation for low voter turnout in this country is due to a combination of both disillusionment and difficulty. How low is voter turnout? In the last 30 years there has been a steady decline. In presidential election years, voter participation has dropped from 62 percent in 1960 to 52 percent in 1980. In off-year congressional elections, it has dropped from 45 percent in 1962 to 35 percent in 1978. These figures mean that a whopping

60 million Americans did not bother to vote in 1980 and that just 26.7 percent of adult Americans elected Ronald Reagan to the White House.

## ACTING RESPONSIBLY

Unfortunately, evangelical registration and voting participation is nearly identical to that of the general public. A 1981 Gallup Poll revealed that 72 percent of evangelicals were registered to vote but a mere 54 percent said that they actually voted in the 1980 election. This means that roughly 10-15 million Christians are not registered to vote. While this is hard to imagine, it reveals just how much citizen education and training needs to take place in the evangelical community.

The Bible is very clear about our responsibility to the society in which we live, and in light of the scriptural mandate for Christians to be involved in the life of the nation, there is no legitimate reason for not voting. Christians should never use the excuse that "I just never got around to it." In order to assist churches in citizen education and training, a simple guide on voter registration is included in the appendix of this book.

Another reason for voting is quite obvious. The Constitution mandates that congressional elections be held every two years. One-third of the senators and all the members of the House of Representatives are elected each election. This means that every two years a new Congress is formed. Consequently, elections force representatives and senators to account for their actions to the voter in their home districts and states.

Members of Congress usually want to be reelected and to do so they must listen to the voters. And voting is the only way possible to ensure the elections of those candidates whose views correspond to our own. So if conscientious, enlightened Christian citizens are sincerely attempting to advance the will of God by exercising their election preferences, the nation cannot help but benefit.

## INFLUENCING HISTORY

Yet some skeptics assert that the value of one vote doesn't make a difference. Evidence points otherwise. Here are a few examples:

In the early 1800s, an Indiana farmer named Shoemaker cast a homemade ballot because the polling place had run out. He voted for Madison Marsh to be his state representative, and Marsh won the election by one vote. In those days, state legislatures elected U.S. Senators. Marsh cast his vote for a man named Harrigan who won the Senate election by one vote. Then, in the Senate, Harrigan cast his vote in favor of Texas's bid for statehood. Texas won by one vote.

That may sound like ancient history, so let us look at the twentieth century. It yields abundant illustrations of narrow-margin victories. In 1916, if Woodrow Wilson had not carried California, he would have lost the presidency to Charles Evans Hughes. Wilson's margin of victory in California amounted to one vote per precinct. In 1948, Lyndon Johnson, running for the Senate, won his first election by 87 votes out of more than 988,000 cast. That secured the political base from which he eventually would become president. Richard Nixon has maintained that in 1960, a shift of 12,000 votes could have given him the presidency over John F. Kennedy.

There are many more such illustrations. And collectively, they reveal how often the direction of history has turned on the narrowest of margins.

## VOTING INTELLIGENTLY

If voting is important, voting intelligently is even more important. Most voters express frustration at the task.

The issues are indeed complex, yet campaigns in this country are not usually designed to educate the voter. As for the candidates, they are not always willing to be vulnerable and reveal much about themselves. Instead, an image is created and put up for sale. Voters are then expected to simply make a psychological purchase of a candidate, apart from any solid information about the voting record of the incumbent or the qualifications of the challenger.

While this is not always true of presidential elections, most polling data shows this to be the case in congressional elections. Incumbency itself, along with the recognition and the positive evaluations it provides, often becomes the most critical factor in the congressional races. This is particularly unfortunate since Congress, not the White House, determines the outcome and direction of public policy on many issues for the nation.

What factors most influence voting decisions? The methods most often used by voters to select candidates are twofold—party label and ideological predisposition. Both of these are unsatisfactory, particularly for Christians. Let's look at the reasons why.

### Party Affiliation

Most voters in this country identify with either the Democratic or Republican parties. A 1981 Gallup poll revealed that 27 percent of the voting public considered itself independent, although a smaller figure would consider itself altogether independent of the two parties. Compared to 15 years ago, the number of voters who claim to be independent has increased, but party identification is still more enduring than many other political attitudes. Factors most likely to alter party voting are political events, economic conditions and the past performance of government leaders.

But to vote simply by party label, as most voters do, is an insufficient basis for casting a vote for any candidate. There are, after all, many differences among politicians of the same party. Additionally, simply voting by party loyalty overlooks the importance of the personal qualifications of each candidate. Since both political parties attempt to manipulate voters with appeals to party labels, with themes of patriotism and with a candidate's charisma, overcoming these blandishments requires a commitment to a different set of voting principles.

## Ideological Predisposition

Voters are also influenced to choose candidates by their own ideological predisposition, whether liberal or conservative. The weaker the effect of party identification, the more important this factor can be in deciding the vote. Ideology, determined largely by certain demographics such as race, ethnicity, income level, education, occupation and age, becomes an important factor in choosing a candidate. A candidate receives a vote if he has made stands on certain issues that appeal to the voter's values or are perceived as "correct."

This method of voting is also woefully inadequate. It, too, overlooks personal qualifications and relies instead on an ideological litmus test. For the Christian, using such a method means that one's political ideology is more important than even biblical principles about what is right or wrong. Such a method puts candidates into an ideological box—either liberal or conservative—and allows the voter to cast a ballot for whichever candidates' ideological predisposition matches their own. This hardly constitutes an intelligent or biblically sound way to vote.

Sociological studies have confirmed this kind of voting behavior. Peter Berger's surveys during the tumultuous 1960s showed that most religious people, ranging from

Unitarian-Universalists to separatistic fundamentalists, voted along social and class lines, rather than according to their professed beliefs. Southern fundamentalists used religious arguments to bolster segregation, while northern fundamentalists attacked it.

## VOTING FAITHFULLY

So, the question arises: What difference should my religious faith have upon the way I vote? It ought to mean, first of all, that we dispense with either party labels or ideological considerations as determining factors in voting for a particular candidate. But doing so will not be easy. While political parties court our votes with slick advertising and emotional appeals, special interest groups press us to vote for candidates that have the so-called "correct" stands on the issues. The strength and number of these groups has grown considerably over the past few years. Here are a few examples:

For years voters have been influenced by lobbies and political action groups that have rated members of Congress by their floor votes and then promoted them on that basis alone. Some of these groups are liberal, such as Americans for Democratic Action (ADA) or the AFL-CIO's political arm, the Committee on Political Education (COPE). Others are conservative, such as Americans for Constitutional Action or the Chamber of Commerce. There are even quasi-religious organizations that publish their own sets of ratings. Bread for the World (BFW) is a liberal hunger lobby that issues a rating of "bread" or "crusts" to legislators, depending upon their votes on food or military programs. Christian Voice is a conservative lobby that publishes a rating chart of members of Congress based upon their votes in certain issues like abortion, prayer in schools, and defense spending.

Voting for candidates based upon such a limited set of

considerations, with the few issues that each group has listed as "moral," is not an intelligent way to select our nation's leaders. What then ought to be considered when choosing a candidate?

## Personal Qualifications

The first criterion for evaluating a candidate ought to be personal qualifications. The reason that personal qualifications are critical is that the attributes of the candidate can have a direct bearing not only on what that person would do in office but also on how successfully those things can be done. While it is difficult to come up with a list of desirable personal qualities, the following ought to be considered:

1. What standard of personal integrity and moral example has the candidate set? A profession of Christian faith ought not to be the sole determining factor in voting for a candidate. While this might be a sign of some permanent values and commitments, it by no means guarantees any political or leadership skills.

2. Does the candidate have any experience and competence in dealing with public issues? This includes being able to make critical decisions, even under intense pressure or in a short period of time.

3. How does the candidate handle a crisis? Look for strength to confront dangers to our national survival, without consideration of personal advantage or image.

4. Does the candidate have a balanced perspective on personal and public responsibility in meeting human needs? Compassion for those impoverished or socially disadvantaged ought to be considered, as should an attitude that the individual has a responsibility to work hard for and contribute to society.

5. Does the candidate keep his campaign promises? Is there a reasonable chance of him meeting a set of short- and long-range goals?

6. With what caliber of associates will the candidate surround himself? Will they be highly qualified or not?

Each of these qualities can be assessed by examining how the candidate has reacted to previous pressures and experiences. Most candidates for public office have held other positions of responsibility either in private business or public service. Make it a point to learn as much as you can.

## Positions on the Issues

Learning the positions the candidates have taken on the issues is another criterion for intelligent voting. And it's important to examine their voting record on all the major issues, not just a select few.* Again, this takes hard work. It means learning what the candidates believe about the issues and deciding which approach is the most likely to succeed. This level of understanding the issues will not come easily, but if we are really serious about influencing public policy, we have no choice. That is the reason this book was written—to encourage Christians to become better informed on a wide range of issues that bear upon the need for basic reform in our society.

To thoroughly evaluate the candidate's record on issues, we must dig below the surface. One member of Congress ventured to speculate that "most evangelical Christians not only are political illiterates but do not spend five minutes a week worrying about it." As a result, he said that they incline toward excessively simplistic judgments because they can't know when Politician A is making sense and Politician B is really insulting their intelligence.

The only cure for making simplistic judgments in the political arena is a heavy dose of political wisdom. But such wisdom cannot simply be imbibed, it is learned and requires study of the issues. Remember, it's possible to receive background information and evidence from national organizations that are active on a subject.

In analyzing issues, you will find a variety of arguments raised. Look for them, or the lack thereof, in the speeches and literature that candidates offer. Four basic kinds of arguments usually emerge: (1) social good: how the proposal will impact people's lives; (2) economics: how much the proposal will cost or save, and what impact it will have on jobs, business, or other financial considerations; (3) ethics: how the proposal will impact on what is morally right or wrong; (4) science and technology: an assertion that certain facts are true or a prediction of what will happen.

It is unlikely that a voter will agree with a candidate on every issue. Hence, some value choices will have to be made about which issues are more important. While the Bible does not give clear, pat answers on every issue, it does provide us with biblical principles. Issues which clearly involve these principles should be given more weight in candidate selection. In analyzing the candidate's arguments also look for different kinds of evidence:

1. Incontestable facts: those that can't be challenged.
2. Contestable facts: those that must be defended.
3. Opinions: the predictions or recommendations of experts and respected people.

## Keeping Informed

In order to understand current events and vote intelligently, we need to be educating ourselves all the time, not just right before an election. Here are some recommendations on keeping informed:

1. Read a daily newspaper—preferably one with a reputation for broad news coverage and fair treatment of public questions. Carefully consider its editorial pages. Do they provide a balanced opinion? Are both liberal and conservative viewpoints represented?
2. Read current event magazines with a variety of viewpoints.
3. Watch television interviews, panel discussions, and documentaries that will help to clarify national and international issues.
4. Go to public meetings on current issues held in your community, including political debates.
5. Read *The Congressional Record* at your public library to discover the thinking of your representatives and senators on currently debated legislation.
6. If your members of Congress send newsletters to their constituents, read them. They frequently provide a good source of ideas for comment.
7. Read a reliable source of information from an evangelical viewpoint.*

An additional word of advice. One of the best ways to stay informed is to become a member of citizen groups active on legislative issues that concern you. Such organizations will help keep you informed through their publications and will tell you when to write to your member of Congress. The big decisions are often inconspicuous details of a bill. If you wait to read about it in your local newspaper, you're unlikely to hear anything until it's all over, because only the final decisions are "news" to most daily papers.

*The NAE public affairs newsletter, *NAE Washington Insight,* offers up-to-date reports on legislative issues of concern to evangelicals. A report of candidates' voting records on all the major issues is also available for a nominal charge from the NAE Office of Public Affairs in the nation's capital.

# 14
# GETTING ORGANIZED

Organizing to influence our society is not something new to Christians. We have been doing it for nearly two centuries now, except in the area of citizen training. This lack is unfortunate since most of the vital concerns raised by the authors of this book require some form of action within the political process. Now is the time to act, and here are some guidelines to get you started. Should some form of citizen's group already exist in your church, this section will help boost its effectiveness.

## IDENTIFY THE NEED

That there is need for citizen training in our churches may be hard for some to imagine. We are inclined to say, "My fellow believers are educated and well-read. Surely they do not need help." But we must recognize that just because a church member is educated and reads the *New York Times* does not necessarily mean that he or she is equipped to tackle public issues. The well-informed citizen will often acquire more facts than skills. He knows more about society than he knows about how to shape or change it.

Studies bear out this fact. The Opinion Research Center and the University of Texas at Austin conducted a study of adult "functional competency" and found a startling amount of "functional illiteracy"—the inability to perform basic tasks which seem essential if one is to cope effectively with modern life. A national sample of 1,500 adults was asked to respond to 67 problems based on real-life situations. Here are some results from the "Government and Law" section:

- When asked to write a letter to a congressman, recommending a vote against a particular bill, 10 percent failed to adequately identify the bill, and 20 percent did not instruct the legislator to vote against the bill.
- When asked whether police have the right to hold an individual for up to a week without bringing charges, 34 percent incorrectly said yes.

Here is some confirming data of a similar nature. Since 1969, an organization called the National Assessment of Educational Progress has been testing a cross-section of young Americans to find out how well the schools are doing. The social studies results are discouraging:

- Less than half of those 17 years old and those 26 to 35 years old understood how to use all parts of a simple ballot.
- Only 60 percent of those 26 to 35 years old understood that presidential candidates are nominated at national conventions.

For whatever reasons, there are many citizenship skills which the schools do not teach. And while studies may have shown that 20 percent of the adult population participates in organized adult education in any given year, less than one percent participate in courses on public affairs, current events or civil issues.

We can see then that many people do not understand how to organize to influence public policy or how our political parties work. It is also safe to assume that they do not know how to analyze the causes of social problems and develop ideas for addressing them. The question for concerned Christians ought to be: "What can we do about this?"

## FORM A CITIZEN'S GROUP

Since you're reading this book, you probably want to do something about these problems. But action without appropriate planning and training can be counterproductive. This is particularly true within the church where active citizenship has not *usually* been stressed. Some Christians are receptive to the idea of forming a citizen training group, but others have doubts. Some of their concerns might parallel those articulated in the introduction of this book.

Be sure to clarify that your method for involvement focuses on Christians as individuals, not on churches as political action groups. You are not seeking to involve the church in politics, but rather Christians as citizens in the political process by exercising the right to vote, contacting decision-makers and conducting study groups on various social concerns, such as those expressed in this book. No one should mistake this kind of response as a disregard for the separation of church and state.

To start off, get together with a handful of people who believe as you do and want to work on an issue. If there is already such an organization within your church, by all means cooperate with them. Quite possibly the way to begin is to set up a committee or a task force as part of the larger committee. When you have formed a citizen's group, keep it informal and encourage others to join. Don't set up a grandiose organization, as that will take up so much time that you'll inevitably find yourself pulled away from the work on the issue.

## CHOOSE A PROJECT

It is important to set an objective before you consider methods or activities. Be specific and start small. Ask yourself, "What is it we want to achieve?" A short-range goal might be to win your congressman's vote on a particular bill. This objective is easily identifiable. A long-range goal might be for every member of your church to be a responsible citizen. While this type of goal is a little hard to quantify, one way to define it is to have 100 percent of the congregation registered to vote and voting; 20 percent of the congregation involved in the political party of their choice; and 10 percent of the congregation actually performing some form of service on behalf of candidates for public office. But do not expect to achieve results overnight. In this case, the first goal must be achieved before the second, and the second before the third. Whatever the objective, it must meet the needs of the congregation or community as well as those of the citizen's group. If it doesn't, the group will flounder and be a waste of time.

## GET EDUCATED TO ACT

Before you decide what action to take on a project it is best to do some preliminary study. This ought to include problem solving. The following five-step model based on the writing of educator John Dewey serves as a set of principles for preparing people to tackle community issues.

### Step 1: Awareness of the Problem

We experience a tension between God's ideal and reality—a problem which motivates us to try to change things. This book has addressed a number of critical issues which fall into this category.

## Step 2: Analysis and Imagination

Attempt to identify and isolate the problem, recall reasons for similar problems and imagine possible solutions. Some models for action have been proposed in this book.

## Step 3: Evaluation of Possible Solutions

Rather than begin a trial-and-error testing of solutions, we use past experience and logic to evaluate the possibilities. The prospect of resolving the problem motivates us to take the next step. There are organizations identified in this book which offer advice based upon prior experiences.

## Step 4: Action

Test the most likely and desirable solution by putting it into action. You'll have to test any particular model or a limited basis in your own unique situation.

## Step 5: Reflection

Assess the results obtained in Step 4, identifying the successful and unsuccessful elements of the process. Store knowledge which can provide for future problem-identification and problem-solving. Why not let the authors of this book know if you tried one of their proposals and found that it worked or did not work?

## UTILIZE SUITABLE RESOURCES

Remember that you do not have to reinvent the wheel or go it alone in your particular project. There is a wealth of assistance within any community that can help a citizen's group to carry out its program. Track down other local groups for encouragement, partnership or even exchange of members and services.

## START NOW

There is a time when every group must stop talking or complaining and start acting. Some groups may be willing to make a commitment to a year, while others may want to try their project first on a limited scale to see if it works. Be flexible and do what works best for you.

Most people involved in running volunteer organizations say that the underlying aims are simple: to find people who can help, to motivate them and to give them responsibility. As your effort grows, you will probably have to move from the original kitchen-table group to a broader division of labor. This is often done by appointing task forces. Don't use the word committee as it has a negative ring to it. But regardless of what you call them, they are set up to perform certain basic functions. Often these functions are research (preparing a factual case), cooperation (building a coalition), membership (recruiting more people) and information (publicity, handouts).

## EVALUATE YOUR PROGRESS

Evaluation merely consists of looking for changes in the project you've undertaken, comparing them with your original goals and deciding whether to reevaluate your methods. Ask yourself, "Are we getting results from what we're doing?" "What contacts have we had with our congressman since our last meeting, and what did he say?" "Did our petition drive bring in any new members or is it losing steam?" "Did our idea of approaching the city council work?"

It is also important to remember that even though your project might not have been identifiably successful in the community, it will likely have had considerable effect upon the lives of the group members or the group as a whole. But if you've had impact upon community, group and individuals, you will know you've accomplished something very worthwhile.

And now, it's up to you to take that first step and get going!

# APPENDIX

# VOTER REGISTRATION—
# A GUIDE FOR
# EVANGELICALS

All the insight and information gained from learning how Congress works does no good unless you are registered to vote. Your member of Congress wants to hear from people who can help him stay in Washington. And if evangelicals are to have an impact upon the government and the course of history, they must exercise their responsibility to vote. Yet many people who are eligible to vote still are not registered. Voter registration drives, then, become an important tool and a good place to start is in your church.

## ASSESS YOUR CHURCH'S NEED . . . NEXT SUNDAY

Why wait? It's easy to assess the need for a voter registration drive in your church. Unless you live in North Dakota where voter registration is not required, you cannot vote without registering your name, address and a few other facts with the necessary officials. It only takes a minute to register.

Most people who have not registered just "never get

around to it." Some may have recently reached age 18. Others may have failed to re-register after moving from another state or community.

Many who believe that they are registered may be shocked on election day to discover that their names have been removed from the rolls. The most common reasons for that are: name change, particularly through marriage; failure to vote in a certain length of time or in the prior general election; registration in another state; or change of address. In certain states, persons who have been convicted of a felony, declared incompetent or committed to a mental hospital may be removed from the rolls. Not all states notify voters when their registrations are cancelled, and even when they do, not everyone reads his mail!

Too, some citizens who know that they are not registered to vote will be ashamed of that fact and may refuse to admit it. It would be helpful if a prominent church member who is currently unregistered would have the courage to acknowledge it publicly and express forcefully why he is going to correct that omission immediately.

Using a Sunday morning worship service to discover who is unregistered demonstrates the importance of voting. We suggest that the pastor take a moment to explain some of the information above, mention the importance of voting and ask for an honest response.

In some churches, it will not embarrass the people to ask those of voting age to stand and then to request those absolutely certain that they are registered to sit down. Those left standing, of course, are the object of the church's voter registration effort. You now have a rough idea of the percentage unregistered, probably at least 25 percent according to most polls. Those still standing should be given a card asking for name, address, home and office telephones. These cards should be collected before the end of the service. This is undoubtedly the most effective way to identify unregistered voters.

In other churches, distributing cards to everyone during the service and asking all who are not positive that they are registered to fill them out may be a more acceptable way. These also should be collected before the service is dismissed.

The procedure can be repeated at services for the next Sunday or two, in men's or women's meetings, in Sunday school classes and in appropriate youth groups.

## BUILD A BIBLICAL CASE . . . IN A SUNDAY SERMON

A skeptic may challenge the appropriateness of registering voters through the church. There is no legal barrier to a nonpartisan voter registration drive, but the protester may suggest that the Bible does not command "Thou shalt vote." Of course not, for such a command would have been irrelevant in the biblical era. The Old Testament people lived in a theocracy. God appointed the leaders and spoke directly to them through His prophets. The people of the New Testament were under the yoke of Rome, with no political rights whatever.

The pastor might well build a practical case for political involvement. Evangelicals must constantly be vigilant to protect their religious liberty, as government entangles itself more and more in the affairs of churches. Our national morality continues to decline, with Judeo-Christian values increasingly excluded from education and legislation. Millions of additional Christians, registering and voting, could give us godly elected officials who would serve both the nation and the will of God. Be advised that those who reject biblical values are hard at work in the election season. Can we afford to be indifferent?

A biblical case will always be the most compelling to evangelical Christians. It should be determinative. The pastor needs to proclaim the scriptural reasons for Christians to be involved in national, state and local elections. He might speak from Psalms 33:12, Proverbs 14:34 or 29:2. He might develop God's command to have dominion over the earth, in Genesis 1:28, or the obligation of Christians to have a proper relationship to government, in Romans 13:1-7, 1 Peter 2:13-17, or 1 Timothy 2:1-4.

The pastor might speak of our Lord's admonition for Christians to be salt, light and yeast, thus permeating and influencing their entire society. He could show what it means to "render unto Caesar," when America's "Caesar" (our highest authority, the Constitution) entrusts us with the responsibility to select our political leaders. What a privilege that is. Men have died for it! The majority of the people on this earth do not have such a God-given opportunity.

America's "noble experiment" produced a marvelous system of self-government. If it is to be truly a representative government, however, evangelicals must not stand aside and let the rest of the population determine who will hold office.

## CHOOSE THE BEST METHOD . . . ALLOWABLE IN YOUR STATE

A telephone call to your city hall or county government should quickly provide basic voter information. Political parties and newspapers can also answer your questions. While it is important to know about residence requirements and deadlines, you mainly need to know how you can assist unregistered friends in your state to become registered. Here are the three basic methods:

1. *Registration by mail.* Twenty-one states currently allow mailed registration cards or forms, and many of them allow anyone to distribute such forms. There is no easier method of voter registration, and it is available to you if

you live in Alaska, California, Delaware, Iowa, Kansas, Kentucky, Maine, Maryland, Minnesota, Missouri, Montana, New Jersey, New York, Ohio, Oregon, Pennsylvania, Tennessee, Texas, Utah, West Virginia, and Wisconsin, plus the District of Columbia.

2. *Registration at your church.* In many states and counties, voter registrars can quickly train and appoint a member of your congregation as a deputy registrar. If that procedure is not permitted, a registrar may be willing to come to your church for a special time of registration. Knowing the number of unregistered voters in your congregation will be useful in showing the benefit of bringing registration into the church.

3. *Registration at official locations.* Registration opportunities are most generally available, the year around, at city halls and county courthouses. Often there are particular election offices. As the dates of elections approach, special satellite locations may be made available by officials in convenient places like shopping malls.

The first and second methods above are the easiest for a church to employ. The third should it be the only method available to you, requires a good deal of publicizing of locations and hours and, to be effective, will require provision of transportation for many members of your church. Perhaps one of your church groups could make it a project.

## DIRECT THE REGISTRATION . . . BEFORE YOUR STATE'S DEADLINE

In 29 states, deadlines for registration run from 28-32 days before election day. Arizona's 50-day registration deadline is the earliest, and four states allow registration on the same day as the election: Maine, Minnesota, Oregon and Wisconsin. The remaining 16 states have miscellaneous deadlines.

We urge you to get a registration program under way

immediately, extending it over several Sundays in order to register as near to 100 percent of the members of your church as possible. Only evangelicals in North Dakota (where no registration is necessary) are excused. It is important to do advance work even in the states which allow election day registration. Use one of these registration methods:

1. *Registration by mail.* Obtain and distribute registration cards to identified non-registered members, and encourage them to complete the cards. Collect and return them to the voter registrar's office or mail the cards individually if that is required. Repeat this process for several Sundays to insure maximum participation.

2. *Registration at your church.* For perhaps four consecutive Sundays, your own deputy registrar(s) or cooperating public official(s) should set up a table in the church foyer or other prime location, for use after Sunday services. The unregistered should be urged not to procrastinate. Whoever is in charge of the process can keep track of those who are unregistered and follow through until all are registered to vote.

3. *Registration at official locations.* Official locations for registration, with days and hours of operation, should be publicized in print and mailed or placed in church bulletins. Working from the card file of unregistered members, the church's voter registration committee may organize special efforts with selected days and times chosen at certain locations. Members can go together on a church bus or be encouraged to appear at a registration site in the same hour. A member of the church can be at each site to provide help. Telephone calls should be made to the unregistered, encouraging them to register so that their vote can be counted in the next election.

Special attention should be given to the problems of those who may be shut in, hospitalized, away on business or otherwise unable to go to the polls on election day. It is important to publicize deadlines and methods for securing absentee ballots for such persons.

## ENLIST OTHER EVANGELICALS . . . AT THE SAME TIME

Pastors or laymen, enthused about the progress and prospects of a voter registration drive in their churches, should share the idea with others. Why not secure a quantity of these brochures from NAE, passing them along personally or by mail? Every evangelical church in your community should have a voter registration drive.

Realizing potential impact of their participation, your church members should want to activate other evangelicals. Here is an optional, creative idea. Prepare some cards for those willing to activate individuals. Let's call it an "Acti-Voters" card. Provide 10 spaces for the names of fellow evangelicals whom they discover to be unregistered and whom they will encourage to become registered. Ask these "Acti-Voters" to report back to the church the number of people they have successfully registered.

## FINISH THE JOB . . . ON ELECTION DAY

Pollsters estimate that 10-15 million evangelicals are currently unregistered to vote. Should all of them exercise their basic citizenship duty to vote intelligently, these evangelicals would have a flavoring and preserving effect on society. After all, we are the salt of the earth, but we cannot permeate our society if we do not get our salt out of the shaker.

While it is unrealistic to expect that 100 percent of evangelicals will vote, such participation would not be necessary to change the course of American history. The Gallup Polls have consistently shown that evangelicals comprise 20 percent of the population in the United States.

Suppose 70 percent of evangelicals voted, while 60 percent of the non-evangelical portion of the population voted? Evangelicals would then have 22.6 percent of the total vote. The impact would be phenomenal.

To illustrate, suppose the bulk of that additional 2.6 percent of the vote had gone toward the losing presidential candidates in 1960 and 1976. Both would instead have won those elections! Richard Nixon would have defeated John F. Kennedy; Gerald Ford would have defeated Jimmy Carter.

Now suppose that the bulk of the evangelical vote in 1980 and 1982 had gone to Democratic senatorial candidates. In 1980, the Republicans would not have gained control of the Senate and the Democratic Party would have continued its 26 year dominance of both Houses of Congress. In 1982, assuming the Republican Senate majority achieved in 1980, that additional vote would have restored control of the Senate to the Democrats.

You see, one of the most common errors in citizens' thinking is the assumption that decisions in this nation are made by a majority of the people. As a matter of fact, never once in the history of this Republic has a majority of all adults elected a president. Just 26.7 percent of voting-age Americans put Ronald Reagan in the White House in 1980, by voting for him. The highest support for any president was given to Franklin D. Roosevelt in 1936, when 34.6 percent of the registered people of voting age voted for him. One hundred years earlier, in 1836, participation was at an all time low when 11.4 percent made Martin Van Buren President.

The above steps will all be to little avail unless the task is finished on election day. Political campaign managers and candidates know how crucial to winning is a get-out-the-vote effort on that critical Tuesday in November.

A committee should carefully divide the entire church

list and by telephone assure that every registered voter actually gets to the polls. Reminder calls may be made the evening before election day. This is the time to discover if anyone needs transportation to the polling place or a baby sitter to allow someone to go to the polls. Volunteers can meet those needs.

The first election day call should be made from 1:00-2:00 in the afternoon, to determine if the voter has voted yet. Those who have should be thanked. Those who have not should graciously be reminded of how important it is that they vote. Midafternoon is a good time to go to the polls, since they will not be as crowded as they are during non-working hours.

A second call could be made to the non-voters from 4:00-5:00. Persistence can pay off, provided callers are courteous. You must reach and persuade your prospective voters. It might be a good idea to have different persons place succeeding calls.

# NOTES

## Chapter 1

1. John Anderson, *Between Two Worlds*, p.15.
2. Interview with George Will, July 14, 1983.
3. John Stott, "Who, Then, Are the Poor?" *Christianity Today* (May 8, 1981), p.55.
4. U.S., Congress, House, Committee on Ways and Means, *Background Material on Poverty*, 17 October, 1983, p.23.
5. Church World Service Immigration and Refugee Program, *Making It On Their Own: From Refugee Sponsorship to Self-Sufficiency*, December 12, 1983, pp.3,5.
6. *Background Material on Poverty*, p.ix.
7. *Ibid*, p.10.
8. *Ibid*, p.4.
9. *Ibid*, p.45.
10. *Ibid*, p.45.
11. *Ibid*, p.128-129.
12. *Ibid*, p.x.
13. J. Larry Brown, Ph.D., Harvard School of Public Health, Testimony Before U.S. House of Representatives, Agriculture Subcommittee on Nutrition, 23 October, 1983.
14. Interview with Ronald J. Sider, June 8, 1984.
15. U.S., Congress, Joint Committee on Taxation, "Federal Tax Treatment of Poor People," reprinted in *Background Material on Poverty*, p.145.
16. Senator Mark O. Hatfield, "Finding the Energy to Continue," *Christianity Today* (February 8, 1980), p.21.
17. George Gilder, *Wealth and Poverty* (New York: Basic Books, Inc., 1981), p.63.
18. *Ibid*, p.68.
19. *Ibid*, p.117.
20. Michael Novak, *The Spirit of Democratic Capitalism* (New York: Simon and Schuster, Inc., 1982), p. 125.
21. Ronald J. Sider, *Rich Christians in an Age of Hunger*

(Downers Grove, Ill: Inter-Varsity Press, 1977), p. 109.
22. Interview with George Will, July 14, 1983.
23. *Ibid.*
24. Senator Jesse Helms, Opening Statement Before U.S. Senate Agriculture Hearing on Private Sector Initiatives, 14 September 1983.
25. John Perkins, *With Justice for All* (Ventura, Calif.: Regal Books, 1982), p.11.
26. Anderson, *op. cit.,* p.153.

## Chapter 3

1. Malcolm Muggeridge, "What the Abortion Argument Is About," *The Human Life Review,* vol. 1, no. 4 (Fall, 1975), p.5.
2. *Roe* v. *Wade,* 410 US 113, 159 This "difficult question," to most observers, was the central issue confronting the Court. Former Watergate special prosecutor Archibald Cox made this point when he wrote: "The opinion fails even to consider what I would suppose to be the most compelling interest of the State in prohibiting abortion: the interest in maintaining that respect for human life which has always been at the center of Western civilization." (Archibald Cox, *The Role of the Supreme Court in American Government,* (New York: Oxford University Press, 1976), pp.51-55, 112-114, 117-118.)
3. U.S., Congress, Senate, Committee on the Judiciary, Subcommittee on Separation of Powers, *Hearing on S. 158,* 97th Congress, 1st sess., 1981, vol. 1, p.14.
4. *Hearing, op. cit.,* p.20.
5. *Hearing, op. cit.,* p.52.
6. *The New Republic,* July 2, 1977, pp.5-6.
7. "A New Ethic for Medicine and Society," *California Medicine,* vol. 113, no. 3 (September 1970). Reprinted in *Human Life Review,* vol. 1, no. 1 (Winter 1975), pp.103, 104.
8. U.S., Congress, Senate, Committee on the Judiciary, Subcommittee on Separation of Powers, Senator John P. East, *Report on When Does Human Life Begin?: Hearing on S. 158,* 97th Congress. 1st sess., 1981, vol. 1, p.11.
9. Peter Singer, "Sanctity of Life or Quality of Life?" *Pediatrics,* vol. 72, no. 1 (July 1983), p.129.
10. John T. Noonan, Jr., "Raw Judicial Power," *National Review* (March 2, 1973, p.261.

11. *Roe* v. *Wade,* 410 US 113, 132. Blackmun was quoting from L. Edelstein, *The Hippocratic Oath,* p.64. Justice Blackmun failed to point out that "ancient religions" also permitted infanticide, torture, crucifixion, slavery, and polygamy, and that it was only through the widespread influence of another "ancient religion," Christianity, that these practices were abolished.

12. *Roe* v. *Wade,* 410 US 113, 162.

13. *Doe* v. *Bolton,* 410 US 179, 221. (This was the companion case to *Roe* v. *Wade.*)

14. Center for Disease Control Abortion Surveillance 1981.

15. God completed His redemptive purposes through the mundane process of childbirth. In the Old Testament mind three parties were active in the birth of every child: the mother, the father and the Holy One. The seemingly endless genealogies of the Bible are replete with meaning for they chronicle the messianic lineage that found its fulfillment in Jesus Christ (Matt. 1:1). At every juncture of God's salvation history, He reminded His people that the seed of promise would fulfill His purposes. In covenant faithfulness, He promised that Eve's seed would crush the head of the serpent (Gen. 3:15), that Abraham's descendants would fill the earth and be God's own possession (Gen. 17:3-8), that the "kinsman-redeemer" would be delivered through the line of Boaz (Ruth 4:13-24), and that David's posterity would establish the kingdom of God forever (2 Sam. 7:12-13).

16. Other portions of Scripture also teach that God creates and fashions each life in the womb. In dialogue with his Creator, Job reminds God of his origins. "Didst Thou not pour me out like milk, and curdle me like cheese; clothe me with skin and flesh and knit me together with bones and sinews" (Job 10:8-11, *NASB*). The Psalmist also acknowledges, "Thy hands made me and fashioned me" (Ps. 119:73, *NASB*), urging his Creator not to "forsake the works of Thy hands" (Ps. 138:8, *NASB*). Scripture, like modern science, also marks conception, when the father's sperm unites with the mother's ovum, as the beginning of an individual life (see 2 Sam. 11:5). "And the woman (Bathsheba) conceived; and she sent and told David, and said, I am with child." (See also 1 Chron. 7:23; Luke 1:36.) Conception is God's gift to humankind, often a direct answer to prayer. "And Isaac prayed to the Lord for his wife, because she was barren; and the Lord granted his prayer, and Rebekah his wife con-

ceived" (Gen. 25:21, *RSV*). Mary's favor with God was marked by the conception of Jesus (Luke 1:30).

17. For a detailed study of prenatal development by a Christian physician see Landrum Shettles and David Rorvik, *The Rites of Life: The Scientific Evidence for Life Before Birth* (Grand Rapids, MI: Zondervan Publishing House, 1983), pp. 25-74.

18. Edward J. Young, *Psalm 139* (London: 1965), p. 72, cited in Donald P. Shoemaker, *Abortion, the Bible and the Christian* (Cincinnati, OH: Hayes Pub. Co., 1978), p. 39. Perhaps the best biblical/theological study on abortion is *Report of the Committee to Study the Matter of Abortion* presented to the 38th General Assembly of the Orthodox Presbyterian Church, May 24-29, 1971.

19. See Graham A.D. Scott, "Abortion and the Incarnation," *Journal of the Evangelical Theological Society* (Winter, 1974), pp. 29-44.

20. *Didache*, ii, 2. For a detailed study of the church fathers on abortion see Michael Gorman, *Abortion and the Early Church*, (Downers Grove, IL: Inter-Varsity Press, 1983).

21. Athenagoras, *Legatio pro Christianis*, P.G. (*Patrologiae Graecae, Cursus Completus*, J.P. Migne, ed.), VI, 970.

22. John Calvin, *Commentaries on the Last Four Books of Moses*, Vol. III, trans. Charles William Bingham (Grand Rapids, MI: William B. Eerdmans Publishing Co., n.d.), pp. 41-42.

23. Dietrich Bonhoeffer, *Ethics*, translated by Neville Horton Smith, (New York: Macmillan Publishing Co., Inc., 1955), p. 131.

24. Karl Barth, *Church Dogmatics*, vol. III, trans. G.W. Bromiley and T.F. Torrance (Edinburgh: T. & T. Clark, 1961), pp. 415ff.

25. Myron S. Augsburger, *Faith for a Secular World*, (Waco, TX: Word Books, 1968), pp. 77-79.

26. C. Everett Koop, *The Right to Live, The Right to Die* (Wheaton, IL: Tyndale House, 1980), pp. 31-35.

27. Cristine Russell, "Physician Group Supports President on Fetus Pain," *The Washington Post* (February, 14, 1984), A6. This article discusses a letter released by a group of 26 physicians, including two past-presidents of the American College of Obstetricians and Gynecologists, supporting President Reagan's statement that fetuses "often feel pain" during abortions. See Stanislav Reinis and Jerome M. Goldman, *The Development of*

*the Brain* (Springfield, IL: Charles C. Thomas Publishing), p.232 and Shettles *op. cit.,* pp.85-93.

28. Liz Jeffries and Rick Edmonds, "Abortion: The Dreaded Complication," *Today,* Philadelphia *Inquirer* (August 2, 1981), p. 17.

29. Mann's entire account of her abortion was read into the Congressional Record by Rep. Chris Smith, 129 *Congressional Record* H7320-22, September 22, 1983.

30. Dick Calvert, *Premature Births and Low Birth Weight Babies in Pregnancies Following an Induced Abortion* and *Repeat Abortion: Its Reproductive Risks* published in 1980 by the Christian Action Council, 422 C St., NE, Washington, D.C. 20002. See also Ann Saltenberger, *Every Woman Has a Right to Know the Dangers of Legal Abortion,* (Glassboro, NJ: Air-Plus Enterprises, 1982).

31. See David Mall and Walter F. Watts, *The Psychological Aspects of Abortion* (Washington, D.C.: University Publications of America, 1979).

32. Norris Magnuson, *Salvation in the Slums,* (Old Tappan, NJ: Scarecrow Press), chapter 6.

33. For information on starting a Crisis Pregnancy Center, write: The Christian Action Council CPC Program, 422 C St., NE, Washington, D.C. 20002.

34. John D. McCarthy, "Social Infrastructures, Deficits and New Technologies: Mobilizing Unstructured Sentiment Pools," unpublished paper, July, 1983, pp.8-10.

35. Karl Barth, *op. cit.,* p.355.

## Chapter 4

1. Often called the Copts, these people account for 10 percent of the population and are not Arabs, but descendants of the ancient Egyptians.

2. Ten percent of the Miskito Indians who form the base of the Moravian church are now refugees in Honduras.

## Chapter 8

1. Ozhigor, S.I. *Slover Ruskogo Yazyka (Dictionary of the Russian Language).* Moscow: Izd. 1981, p. 312.

2. S. Sanakoyev, "Public Forces and Disarmament," *Interna-*

*tional Affairs* (October, 1982), p. 20.

3. Georgi Dimitrov, *Selected Speeches and Articles.* (London: Lawrence and Wishart, 1951), pp. 166, 175.

4. N. Kutikov, "On Just and Unjust Wars," *Soviet Military Review* (March, 1977), p. 8.

5. Milovidovand Kozlov, *The Philosophical Heritage of V. I. Lenin,* Problems of Contemport War, (Washington, D.C.: Government Printing Office, 1975).

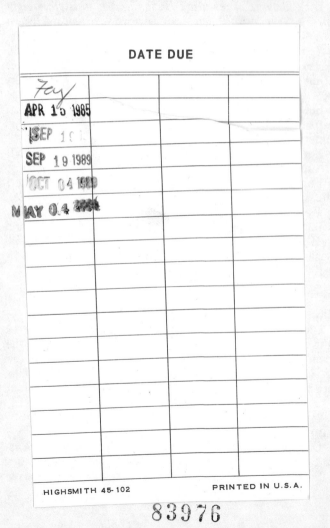

DATE DUE

| | | | |
|---|---|---|---|
| *Fay* | | | |
| APR 15 1985 | | | |
| SEP 1 0 | | | |
| SEP 1 9 1989 | | | |
| OCT 04 1989 | | | |
| MAY 04 | | | |

HIGHSMITH 45-102                    PRINTED IN U.S.A.

83976